T0316542

Cambridge Elements

Elements in the Archaeology of Europe
edited by
Manuel Fernández-Götz
University of Edinburgh
Bettina Arnold
University of Wisconsin–Milwaukee

ARCHAEOLOGY AND THE GENETIC REVOLUTION IN EUROPEAN PREHISTORY

Kristian Kristiansen
University of Gothenburg

CAMBRIDGE
UNIVERSITY PRESS

University Printing House, Cambridge CB2 8BS, United Kingdom

One Liberty Plaza, 20th Floor, New York, NY 10006, USA

477 Williamstown Road, Port Melbourne, VIC 3207, Australia

314–321, 3rd Floor, Plot 3, Splendor Forum, Jasola District Centre,
New Delhi – 110025, India

103 Penang Road, #05–06/07, Visioncrest Commercial, Singapore 238467

Cambridge University Press is part of the University of Cambridge.

It furthers the University's mission by disseminating knowledge in the pursuit of
education, learning, and research at the highest international levels of excellence.

www.cambridge.org
Information on this title: www.cambridge.org/9781009228688
DOI: 10.1017/9781009228701

First published 2022

A catalogue record for this publication is available from the British Library.

ISBN 978-1-009-22868-8 Paperback
ISSN 2632-7058 (online)
ISSN 2632-704X (print)

Archaeology and the Genetic Revolution in European Prehistory

Elements in the Archaeology of Europe

DOI: 10.1017/9781009228701
First published online: August 2022

Kristian Kristiansen
University of Gothenburg

Author for correspondence: Kristian Kristiansen,
Kristian.Kristiansen@archaeology.gu.se

Abstract: This Element was written to meet the theoretical and methodological challenge raised by the third science revolution and its implications for how to study and interpret European prehistory. The first section is therefore devoted to a historical and theoretical discussion of how to practice interdisciplinarity in this new age and, following from that, how to define some crucial but undertheorized categories, such as culture, ethnicity, and various forms of migration. The author thus integrates new results from archaeogenetics into an archaeological frame of reference to produce a new and theoretically informed historical narrative – one that invites further debate and also identifies areas of uncertainty where more research is needed.

Keywords: archaeology, genetics, European prehistory, migration, ethnicity

ISBNs: 9781009228688 (PB), 9781009228701 (OC)
ISSNs: 2632-7058 (online), 2632-704X (print)

Contents

1 Introduction and Background
A Brief History of Research

Right now, archaeology is experiencing its third science revolution (Kristiansen 2014b), which like the previous two is reshaping our entire archaeological discourse (Sørensen 2017a and 2017b; Ribeiro 2019). Common to all three revolutions – the Darwinian revolution introducing to archaeology principles of stratification, deep time, and evolution (1850–60); the environmental revolution and the carbon-14 (C-14) revolution introducing absolute dating (1950–60); and now the strontium/DNA revolution introducing to archaeology prehistoric population genomics and migrations (2010–20) – is the transformation of previous relative knowledge intoabsolute knowledge.[1] In doing so, they freed intellectual resources to be spent on explaining change rather than describing and debating it (Figure 1). Thus, prior to the C-14 revolution, most archaeological resources were poured into the classification and relative dating of prehistoric cultures. Beyond the safe dates of written sources, one had to project back in time the supposed length of time periods based on stratigraphy and typology. As we now know, all prehistoric periods earlier than the Bronze Age turned out to be much older than anticipated. Once the C-14 revolution unfolded and thousands of dates established safe chronologies, intellectual resources could instead be spent on explaining change, leading on to New Archaeology and what followed. Thus, these science revolutions were also intellectual revolutions propelling archaeological theory and interpretation forward.

In order to better understand and evaluate the present situation, it can be useful to trace the history of interdisciplinarity in archaeology through an analysis of the three science revolutions, and their transformative potential, and also the commonalities between all three revolutions, their theoretical and methodological implementation, and their impact on archaeology.

The Birth of Archaeology and the First Science Revolution

Archaeology as a discipline was born out of interdisciplinary collaboration. It happened during the crucial decade of 1850 to 1860, when the new natural sciences of geology, biology, and zoology achieved breakthroughs precisely through interdisciplinary collaboration with archaeology. In turn, archaeology achieved its status as an independent discipline through interdisciplinary

---

[1] This does not imply that there is no debate possible about interpretation or improvement of methodologies. A good historical example is the calibration curve of C-14; similarly, one can also discuss the way aDNA data is analyzed and presented using different statistical methods. However, the baseline is that certain types of questions can be answered with a high degree of probability and that genetic base data is correct, if correctly sequenced.

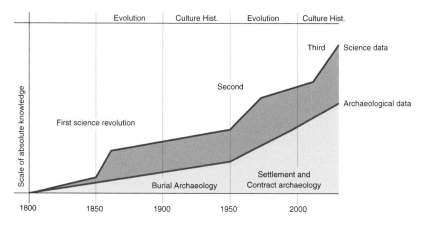

Figure 1 Model of the impact of the three science revolutions in archaeology through their transformation of relative knowledge to absolute knowledge

collaboration with zoology and geology. It happened through the combined application of systematic excavation, observation, and documentation in the three disciplines (Kristiansen 2002; Grayson 1983).

Excavation and classification were thus the new methodological principles in archaeology borrowed from geology, zoology, and biology (the work of Charles Darwin and Carl Linné), which propelled it into an independent discipline. Classification and typology were further developed by Oscar Montelius to become the new methodological tools of archaeology; and in anthropology, the concept of evolution inspired a new perception of the social evolution of human culture in the works of Lewis H. Morgan (*Ancient Society* [1877]) and E. B. Tylor (*Primitive Culture* [1871]).

The decade of 1850 to 1860 thus revolutionized the classical biblical perceptions of the antiquity of Man and laid the foundations not only for the modern worldview, but also for its science-based foundations in geology, zoology, and archaeology. We can hardly imagine the revolutionary impact of these discoveries during their time. They became an essential part of the birth of modernity and a new perception of history and science (Toulmin and Goodfield 1965; Grayson 1983; Schnapp 1996; Schnapp and Kristiansen 1999).

The Second Science Revolution: The Birth of Environmental Science and Absolute Time

Two apparently unrelated scientific breakthroughs during the 1940s and 1950s transformed archaeology into a modern science-based discipline, which fostered a massive theoretical and interpretative development during the 1960s onward in the form of "New Archaeology." The two breakthroughs were (1) the development of modern pollen analysis and environmental archaeology; and (2) the development of C-14 absolute dating, which completely changed the dating of prehistory before written sources.

The implications of the C-14 method for absolute archaeological dating were revolutionary, especially for periods before written sources. It turned out that the Neolithic and Chalcolithic periods in particular were several thousand years older than had been suggested by extrapolating from the known to the unknown – from the safe dates of the Bronze Age and back in time. However, most of this extrapolation turned out to be wrong. This meant that the whole chronological framework for prehistory before the Bronze Age collapsed and – along with it – its interpretative framework, based on the diffusion of farming and early metallurgy from the Near East. Colin Renfrew was among the first to use this to propose a new interpretative framework, where autonomous development became a dominant explanatory framework for much of European prehistory. New theoretical models were applied to support this new framework, under the banner of processual or New Archaeology, summarized by Renfrew in his book *Before Civilisation: The Radiocarbon Revolution and Prehistoric Europe* (Renfrew 1973). Processual archaeology employed a comparative approach, where ethnographic models in particular were mobilized to show that human societies worldwide were characterized by parallel and independent social evolution and innovation, in works by Elman Service (1962 and 1975) and Marshall Sahlins (1972). However, archaeological infrastructures also developed rapidly during this period, as well as the methodological and theoretical framework, by gradually including historical and contemporary archaeology as well (Kristiansen 2008, figure 1.3).

Thus, during the 1940s and 1950s, natural sciences took a giant step forward with the development of high-resolution pollen analysis and of C-14 dating, followed by a series of new analytical techniques, which created a whole new framework for archaeological theory and practice. In conjunction with the increasing emphasis on settlement archaeology and the role of contract archaeology in modern society (Cleere 1984, 1989), the consequences turned out to be dramatic in the period after 1960. It led to a restructuring not only of theory and practice, but also of the whole organizational framework of archaeology and of its role in society. New science departments for pollen analysis, paleobotany, and C-14 dating were created at many universities and national museums around the world. Natural science – or rather archaeoscience –was from now on implemented in teaching, fieldwork, and research as a matter of routine.

The Third Science Revolution: The Births of Archaeogenetics and Big Data

The third science revolution has been unfolding since 2010, but its beginnings were much earlier. Ammerman and Cavalli-Sforza (1984) were among the first to take advantage of the initial genetic breakthrough of mitochondrial DNA in the early 1980s, in an attempt to use modern genetic data to infer prehistoric migrations (discussed in Reich 2018, introduction). Soon it became possible to extract mitochondrial DNA from ancient samples, although this only contains a fraction of the genetic evidence, linked to the female lineage. A first wave of optimism was soon replaced by pessimism, as it turned out that contamination from present-day human DNA had become a nearly unsolvable problem. It was only after the publication of the first full human genome in 2004 and the development of short-read sequencing technologies that ancient DNA (aDNA) genome research became a reality, with the first prehistoric genomes published in 2010 by the Copenhagen team (Rasmussen et al. 2010) and the Max Planck team (Green et al. 2010). Since then, we have seen a steeply rising curve of new data, as well as new results that have changed the perception of prehistory globally (summarized in popular books by Reich [2018] and Krause [2019]). This has been followed by an extensive popular dissemination of results, sometimes in a more sensational form than wished for.

Another side of the third science revolution is its powerful use of big data. Once archaeological data entered the digitized world, it could be analyzed and correlated with other types of data, such as the geodata forming the backbone of GIS (McCoy 2017) or environmental and genetic data (Racimo et al. 2020a and 2020b; Roberts et al. 2018). All published genetic data is stored in a global database. This means that all new aDNA analyses can be compared to previous analyses, as well as to modern reference data. Old data can in this way be reanalyzed with new methods, all of which is part of the rapid advance and strength of archaeogenetics.

So far, most archaeological big data is stored in national databases and is therefore of limited use. Thus, the full potential of archaeological big data has yet to be realized (Huggett 2020; Perry and Taylor 2018). However, lists of C-14 dates have been made publicly available in the journal *Radiocarbon* since 1959 and can thus be employed in more advanced research crosscutting national borders. Such research has already had a profound effect upon our understanding of prehistoric demography (Hinz et al. 2012; Shennan et al. 2013; Blanko-Gonzales et al. 2018; Roberts et al. 2019).

The third science revolution is now slowly entering the implementation phase, as its results become more widely acknowledged, in tandem with a rapidly increasing number of prehistoric genomes, which allow the unfolding of much more detailed human and social histories. To better understand where we are in the process between breakthrough and implementation, I shall illuminate such processes more generally.

The Process of Scientific Breakthroughs

Historically, it can be demonstrated that major advances in archaeological interpretation are based on the results of interdisciplinary collaboration and breakthroughs. Perhaps it is the mere challenge produced by interdisciplinary research that holds the key to its innovative power, by forcing us to perceive the past in new, unexpected ways, in combination with the transformation from relative to absolute knowledge that each science revolution brought about, and which has continuously freed intellectual resources to be spent on interpretation and explanation rather than documentation.

What more can we learn from the history of interdisciplinarity to better understand the ongoing third science revolution? Based on observations from the three science revolutions in archaeology, we can define a three-step process in the formation and implementation of science revolutions: (1) An upstart phase or prologue when new methods and new knowledge are being formulated and tested, yet without a clear perception of their scientific potential. This is realized in (2) the breakthrough phase, when suddenly a leading researcher or research group demonstrates the full potential of the new methods. This is then followed by (3) an implementation phase, where methods become standardized and widely applied. I shall next describe the commonalities of these three phases.

Prologue

This is the phase from the detection of a new scientific field or principle to its full application. It normally lasts around twenty-five years. Twenty-five years passed from the detection of pollen to its application as a science of human impact on the environment, and another ten years before enough pollen types had been identified to allow full environmental reconstruction. Twenty-five years passed between the first detection and analysis of human DNA and its full genomic application in aDNA. Likewise, twenty-five years passed from the detection of stratified geological layers to their combination with archaeological and zoological documentation and classification.

Breakthrough

This is when one or more leading research groups are able to demonstrate the full potential of the new scientific principles, by recombining them into a new methodological package, as happened during the first science revolution, or when a scientific method can be applied in a new field, as happened when C-14 determination and pollen analysis were applied to archaeological data, or when new powerful computers in combination with new methods of sorting contamination led to the breakthrough of next-generation sequencing of ancient DNA. Along the way from breakthrough to implementation, one can often observe an intermediate phase of doubt and critique, where critical methodological adjustments are made (Figure 2). For the C-14 method, it is represented by the phase leading to calibration, and right now strontium isotopic research is going through a similar phase as to how to establish reliable baselines. It might be proposed that aDNA went through an analogous process during the early 2000s, when disillusion due to contamination problems nearly killed the field, before leading up to next-generation sequencing.

Implementation

This is when the new results and their methods become widely accepted and routinized. This is also when their interpretative and theoretical implications are fully understood and applied, sometimes leading to the formation of new disciplines. During the first science revolution, archaeology, geology, and zoology reached their final form as scientific disciplines, just as zoological and archaeological museums and research departments were established all over the world. Now, the traditional field of zoology is part of archaeological laboratories, while genetics has taken over basic research in biological evolution. Likewise, pollen botanical analysis became part of a new biological subdiscipline, today partly superseded by environmental DNA, and commercial

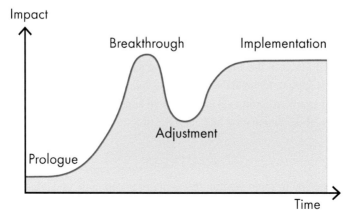

Figure 2 Model of the process of scientific breakthroughs

C-14 laboratories were established from the late 1950s onward. The third science revolution is so far contained within the confines of basic university research, with publications in high-profile journals, but is supported by widespread publicity in the press. While we witness an expansion of aDNA laboratories around the world, the scientific leaders are still a handful of university-based research institutions. The field has not yet entered the implementation phase.

However, we may also observe another historical regularity following the three science revolutions, which I shall term culture-historical counterrevolutions.

Revolutions and Counterrevolutions

Counterrevolutions can be defined as a discursive reaction from practitioners of humanities and cultural history against science-based interpretations, or rather about the role of science, which in their view should be supporting archaeological interpretation rather than playing an equal, collaborative role – if it has a role at all. It is well described and discussed by Martinon-Torres and Killick (2015). Early postprocessualists especially were hostile toward science and wanted to abolish science and quantification, as they "dehumanized" history, in the words of Shanks and Tilley (1987a, 77). However, the trend was partly reversed by the example of the Çatalhöyük project led by Ian Hodder, synthesized in Hodder (1992). Now, we witness a similar critical debate over the role of big data and quantitative modeling versus contextual studies (Huggett 2020; Ribeiro 2019).

These debates, or counterrevolutions, have accompanied archaeology from the very beginning, leading to repeated swings of the pendulum at intervals of thirty to fifty years (Figure 3). Since the beginnings of the discipline, there has existed a debate over the relationship between archaeology and science, which has led to a number of ontological turns that I termed "Rationalism" and "Romanticism" (Kristiansen 1996, figure 4, 2008, figures 2 and 7). Should archaeology be a historical discipline whose interpretations were anchored in a humanistic discourse of the particular, or a science-based discipline whose interpretations were anchored in a scientific discourse of historical regularities? For every discursive turn, however, the repertoire of archaeology expanded, and even if the dominant interpretations were sometimes one-sided, new methods – from excavation techniques to science-based analyses – steadily expanded the archaeological field of knowledge and thus paved the way for the next revolution. Each revolution in turn responded to the previous one: The culture-historical turn after 1900 was a reaction against the dominantly grand schemes of typology and social evolution, leading to a new focus on local culture histories and the identification of ethnic groups with material cultures as represented by the

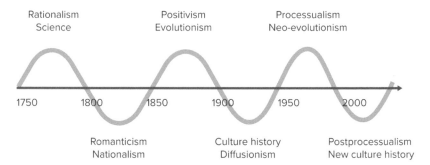

Figure 3 Graph showing repeated swings of the historical pendulum between the two dominant discourses: the science-based, and the humanistic-based, corresponding broadly to the "Two Cultures" in the terminology of C. P. Snow

Kossinna school in European archaeology, the related "Kulturkreislehre" of the Vienna school in ethnography, and the Boas school in the USA. New Archaeology was the predictable counterrevolution against this interpretative scheme, supported by the second science revolution, which in turn spurred a "reactionary" (in the words of Ian Hodder [1982a]) culture-historical counter-revolution that became postprocessualism, which was linked to the postmodern turn in humanities and social sciences. And now the historical pendulum is swinging again with the third science revolution (Kristiansen 2014b).

Throughout all of these revolutions and counterrevolutions, archaeology expanded its repertoire of methods and theories. Therefore, archaeology embraces more diversity than probably any other discipline, both in terms of time depth – from the Paleolithic to the present – and in terms of materials, methods, and theories. Progress in interpretation and new knowledge likewise come from many directions (Lucas 2015 and 2017; Sørensen 2018) – from revisiting old material in museum stores or more likely today from compiling such material in new accessible databases with the potential of big data analysis. It comes from revisiting old philosophical and theoretical positions in the humanities, social sciences, and philosophy, which are constantly updated, from hermeneutics to social evolution (Gardner, Lake and Sommer 2013). And it comes from new breakthroughs in science, such as strontium isotopic tracing of mobility and next-generation sequencing of aDNA, which has suddenly allowed genomic analyses of prehistoric individuals. It revitalized old collections of human remains in museums, just as new methods of lead isotopic analysis revitalized collections of bronzes or lipid analysis revitalized pots and potsherds. More than 150 years of systematic collecting pays off when new observations and new scientific methods can be applied to old materials. Therefore excavators, museum curators, scientists, and theoretical archaeologists are all unified in maintaining this complex web of stored information that is the infrastructure of archaeology, and whose knowledge potential has always demanded interdisciplinarity. Throughout its history, archaeology has been dominated by one or the other interpretative perspective – science or humanities – and in the best of worlds by their collaboration, most often when the historical pendulum was in a middle position on its way from one to the other discourse – the position where we are right now (Figure 3).

Archaeology is thus a creative, borrowing discipline, which has throughout its history successfully applied many methods and theories from a variety of disciplines, from social anthropology, history, and philosophy to various branches of science from geology, zoology, and physics to genetics. Therefore, archaeology is interdisciplinary, or it is nothing.

Archaeology and Genetics: An Ongoing Debate about Interpretation

The Current Debate

As would be expected, a revolution does not unfold without critique, even opposition, as well as debate about how to understand and interpret its results. These debates, however, besides being necessary, are also informative about the dynamics of adapting to a new scientific reality. Here, I shall concentrate on methodological and theoretical aspects and leave the debate about ideology to the next section.

I take inspiration from three thoughtful contributions in order to contextualize the debate. At the recent 9th ISBA Conference on Biomolecular Archaeology in Toulouse (June 2021), the keynote talk by Tamsin O'Connell discussed what is real and unreal in current debates on interdisciplinarity. To unravel the process, she returned to David Clarke's classic paper "Archaeology: The Loss of Innocence" (Clarke 1973). Here, he focuses on the big transitions in archaeology, and he outlines the historical process from being "conscious," to becoming "self-conscious," before reaching the phase of "critical self-consciousness." Tamsin O'Connell then suggested that the current transition of the third science revolution can be described by applying this framework. She concluded that, from the perspective of biomolecular archaeology, we were still in the phase of being "self-conscious." It implies that the ability to take critique on board is still considered threatening to the newly won consciousness of biomolecular archaeology. The conclusion was that too much is at stake to reach a more mature level of "critical self-consciousness" at the present moment. Why is that? In order to understand this phenomenon, we need to focus on the meaning and demands of being interdisciplinary. Then it becomes more comprehensible.

In a recent paper, Liv Nilsson Stutz suggests that, in order to create a more productive environment for interdisciplinary collaboration, it is necessary to understand what it takes and that it represents a demanding process of increasing knowledge-sharing. She then suggests a three-phase knowledge- sharing process, moving from "multidisciplinarity," through "interdisciplinarity" toward "transdisciplinarity" (Stutz 2018). She defines the different stages in the following way. *Multidisciplinarity* denotes a model where different disciplines, each providing its own perspective, collaborate by bringing their disciplinary expertise to bear on an issue. *Interdisciplinary* work denotes a higher level of integration by analyzing, synthesizing, and harmonizing links between disciplines "into a coordinated and coherent whole." Finally, *transdisciplinarity*, even more integrated, creates a unity of intellectual frameworks beyond the disciplinary perspectives. I suggest combining the two perspectives into a single processual model (Figure 4).

However, there exists a third level of potential misunderstanding between disciplines in interdisciplinary research collaborations, which has been identified by Alexandra Ion in a recent contribution (Ion in press). She states:

> There might be two main challenges inherent to the fact that the data is very different in nature: (1) each discipline might have its own ontological reading of the studied object; (2) the scale the data operates on. For these reasons when different disciplines meet on the same territory either tensions or misunderstandings might arise (see article on terminology by Eisenmann et al. 2018). In the case of genetic analysis, osteology, cultural anthropology, isotope studies etc., each of them has their own ontological view ascribed to "a person's identity."

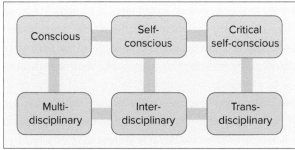

Degree of disciplinary consciousness

Degree of interdisciplinarity

Figure 4 Model of the proposed relationship between degree of disciplinary consciousness in archaeology and degree of interdisciplinarity

She rightly suggests that the impact of different ontologies has been somewhat overlooked: "Surprisingly though, it seems that precisely this complex process of negotiation and of finding a 'meta-language' is almost absent at present." (Ion 2019: 177, 189, see also Sørensen 2017a and 2017b for earlier discussion).

To situate the present debates, we need to understand the ultimate goal of transdisciplinarity. According to Liv Nilsson Stutz, it is a way of integrating all the different voices inside and outside academia that form our perceptions of the past – from cultural, critical heritage to the way we interpret evidence under a shared theoretical framework that understands the complicated processes of genetics and culture interactions – and which are able to situate the results in the present. We are certainly not there yet, rather we are in the middle phase where the two disciplines are grappling to create a shared understanding of genetic and archaeological evidence and their impact in the present. Here, archaeology comes with the burden of a long history of contested and sometimes politicized narratives of the past against a new genetic discipline of aDNA without such a historical burden. This imbalance has clearly shaped some of the debates about European prehistory.

I venture to propose that right now we are in a phase where sometimes misunderstanding, even misrepresentation, of "the other" has led to a series of partly unfounded critiques, or rather overinterpretations, of what new genetic results imply from both sides. It is also in some measure due to the kind of misunderstanding that Ion ascribed to different metalanguages: Geneticists have a specific understanding of genetic admixture and change that cannot easily be translated into archaeological language without simplification. As a result, critical archaeologists have tended to overstate the negative interpretative implications or dangers of at least some genetic results, while some genetic papers on the contrary have tended to overinterpret their results in terms of archaeological and linguistic implications.

One example of the latter, which kickstarted the debate, was a paper by Haak et al. from 2015, which stated that "Massive migration from the steppe was a source for Indo-European languages in Europe." Here, we have a title that went beyond the purely genetic implications of the results presented and proposed wide-ranging implications for how Indo-European languages spread that were not sustained by the actual results in the paper.[2] It is interesting to note, though,

---

[2] Hidden away deep down as Supplementary Information 11 (SI11), with the title "Relevance of ancient DNA to the problem of Indo-European language dispersals," we find a debating text of some importance, as it contains a rather detailed discussion of the various hypotheses for Indo-European language origins and presents a much more detailed series of arguments. It states: "While our results do not settle the debate about the location of the proto-Indo European homeland, they increase the plausibility of some hypotheses and decrease the plausibility of others." Then, each of the four hypotheses is discussed, which is followed by a discussion about "Pitfalls in using genetic data to make inferences about language spread." It starts with a carefully

that the discussion text is rather more cautious in its wording about linguistic implications:

> Our results provide new data relevant to debates on the origin and expansion of Indo-European languages in Europe (SI11). Although ancient DNA is silent on the question of the languages spoken by preliterate populations, it does carry evidence about processes of migration which are invoked by theories on Indo-European language dispersals. Such theories make predictions about movements of people to account for the spread of languages and material culture. The technology of ancient DNA makes it possible to reject or confirm the proposed migratory movements, as well as to identify new movements that were not previously known.

Then the two prevailing hypotheses are mentioned, and it is suggested that the new results challenge the Anatolian hypothesis, but also "we caution that the location of the Proto-Indo-European homeland that also gave rise to the Indo-European languages of Asia, as well as the Indo-European languages of southeastern Europe, cannot be determined from the data reported here." The temptation to oversell the results in a catchy title provoked debate, in retrospect perhaps useful.

The paper demonstrated that a major genetic replacement took place after 3000 BC in Europe, with lasting effects into the present genetic composition of Europe's populations. These results were supported by the paper by Allentoft et al. from 2015 published in the same issue of *Nature* with the more neutral title "Population Genomics of Bronze Age Eurasia." Taken together, the two papers implied that a population replacement of some magnitude took place within a relatively limited time span, at least in archaeological terms. However, the historical-archaeological implications of how and why it actually happened remained to be detailed.

In the debate that followed, archaeology's burdensome historical heritage was once again mobilized as a warning against overtly simplistic interpretations, implied by the title of a paper by Volker Heyd, "Kossinna's Smile"

---

worded section about the role of Kossinna and his hypotheses, and the text concludes: "Although in this study we have focused on the genetic findings, our data are also interesting from the point of view of archaeological methodology. Specifically, our findings challenge the idea of a limited role of migration in human population history by providing unambiguous evidence of two major episodes of migration and population turnover in Europe. By documenting not only that these major migrations occurred, but that they were both followed to a degree by the genetic resurgence of the local populations (SI7, Fig. 3), we hope that our study will help to spur new debate on the interactions between migrants and indigenous peoples long after the occurrence of migration." It certainly did, but I wonder how many archaeological readers found their way to this much more cautious but hidden away supplementary text. It reveals that a debate among the coauthors took place, and only some of the more cautious wording found its way into the main text, but not into its title.

(2017). While generally positive to the results, which supported much of his own previous research, he took issue with the simplistic interpretation of "large scale migrations" from Yamnaya to Corded Ware, since it ignored the complexity of the archaeological record. Thus, there is a 150-year-long chronological standstill from Yamnaya to the formation of Corded Ware, and, more importantly, Yamnaya represents a steppe economy, while Corded Ware represents a mixed farming economy with pastoral ingredients. How to account for the transformation from one to the other? Finally, he pointed to earlier contacts during the fourth millennium BC between the Caucasus/steppe and central Europe, which might potentially have brought some migrants along as well and paved the way for the sudden transformation. He thus mobilized the archaeological record to show that central questions remained unanswered (see also the debate in Furholt 2018 with comments).

Like the *Nature* editor, who decided to publish two supporting papers in the same issue in 2015, so did the editor of *Antiquity* decide to bring two complementary papers together in the same issue, one critical (Heyd 2017), the other interpretative (Kristiansen et al. 2017). The latter presented new theoretical and interpretative models for the steppe migrations and how they shaped the Corded Ware culture, as well as changing the linguistic landscape. The paper also integrated results from strontium isotopic research with genetic and archaeological results, which allowed the reconstruction of kinship and marriage patterns (further Knipper et al. 2017). It also presented for the first time concrete linguistic evidence that supported the steppe hypothesis for the spread of Indo-European languages, based on research done by Guus Kroonen (also Iversen and Kroonen 2017).

We have since then witnessed a productive discussion about how to detail and understand migratory processes in European prehistory, most prominently in papers by Martin Furholt (2018, 2019, and 2021). These contributions have stressed the multilayered foundations of cultural and social change, with burial rituals as a shared foundational trait, while material culture is more varied and is gendered (Bourgeois and Kroon 2017; Stockhammer 2022).

The interdisciplinary model from Kristiansen et al. (2017) has by now become a new standard, producing convincing results as to the reconstruction of kinship systems, as well as social stratification (Mittnik et al. 2019, Sjögren et al. 2021). More recently, we have also seen how environmental data has been integrated into interpretations of the Corded Ware migrations, opening up the possibility of much more regional variation (Haak et al. 2022). Increasingly, we witness the combination of micro and macro studies, which opens up a more complex understanding of forces of change, and not least the rules governing such changes, from kinship systems to environmental change. It provides an answer to previous critiques of simplistic grand narratives in the early phase of the genetic revolution (Furholt 2018; Ion 2019).

The Way Forward

A way forward for archaeology is thus to reclaim the interpretative lead rather than to critique, and such a strategy is now beginning to impact the field, notably through works by Martin Furholt (2019 and 2020), as well as Booth, Brück, Brace, and Barnes (2020). They demonstrate the importance of archaeological contexts, and the way they may impact on the interpretation of genetic evidence, from burial evidence to other forms of rituals. Booth, Brück, Brace, and Barnes have been digging through the supplementary archaeological information of the Bell Beaker paper (Olalde et al. 2018), providing new evidence of more complex processes during the adaptation to new social circumstances after settling down in the British Isles. Similarly, a recent paper by Armit and Reich reformulated the arrival of steppe ancestry into the British Isles into two possible hypotheses: one that allowed an "invisible" earlier gradual spread and one that corresponded to the arrival of the Beaker culture package (Armit and Reich 2021). Focus is thus increasingly upon the social and cultural nature of genetic admixture processes. We have likewise seen more localized genetic and archaeological studies of the arrival of steppe ancestry into Bohemia, which again revealed more complex processes of genetic and cultural transmission and admixture (Papac et al. 2021).

The Danger of Ideological Misrepresentation

Due to archaeology's historical heritage of political misuse, some archaeologists fear that the current revolution in the study of aDNA will again invite simplistic racist equations of culture, people, and language, as in the past. In the prewar period, the prehistoric spread of the Indo-European languages was increasingly attributed to the superiority of an alleged Indo-European-speaking ethnolinguistic unity, which – despite all linguistic evidence to the contrary – was claimed to have developed, since the Neolithic, in North Europe. Through the *Siedlungsarchaeologie* of Gustaf Kossinna (1858–1931), the question of Indo-European linguistic origins was integrated into nationalist theories on German ethnic origins. But similar ethnic interpretations were widespread in both archaeology and ethnography (Demoule 2012; Hansen 2019). It is very well possible that future interdisciplinary studies will again lead to misinterpretations that are liable to political abuse. Here, we should mention the rise of an out-of-India model of Indo-European languages during the previous generation, primarily motivated by Hindu nationalism. These are the same kind of forces that used the model of Gustaf Kossinna to support a Nazi racist ideology nearly 100 years earlier. The out-of-India model has been firmly rejected by recent results from aDNA (Narasimhan et al. 2019), and it has little or no support among the historical linguistic research environment (cf. Witzel 2012). However, it should serve as a warning example of the political impact of nationalism in the present as well, of which several examples can be cited (Shnirelman 2001, Díaz-Andreu and Champion 1996).

The most obvious risks of ideological misrepresentation occur when such forces infiltrate the academic environment, as happened in Germany during the Nazi regime. But the risk of such abuse will likely only increase if relevant evidence is ignored rather than welcomed. If there is anything that the recent interdisciplinary biomolecular studies have shown, it must be that the once-dominant Eurocentric and supremacist perspectives on the Indo-European home-land are not supported by any genetic or linguistic evidence. According to aDNA, all Europeans have been subject to the same genetic admixture processes, and thus there is no genetic support for such narratives. On the contrary, all Europeans belong to the same genetic stock or "family," a message that has been communicated in popular books by geneticists, science journalists, and others (Bojs 2017; Krause 2019; Reich 2018).

In addition, modern DNA research raises fundamental questions about what it means to be human (Barrett 2014), what genetic variation means, what archaeological cultures mean (Furholt 2019 and 2020; Roberts and Vander Linden 2011), and the prospects of such knowledge for ideological propaganda, whether racist or antiracist, nationalist or antinationalist (Hakenbeck 2019; Frieman and Hofmann 2019). In short, it demands a stronger public engagement by archaeologists, scientists, and humanists, perhaps to a degree we are not used to. Therefore, we need to engage in the ways new results are disseminated in the public domain (Källen et al. 2019), whether by writing popular books and articles or by engaging with science journalists, as their articles reach a wide readership. The past has always been exploited for political purposes, for good and ill (Díaz-Andreu 2007). One of the most destructive political misuses of the past has been for the construction of nationalist narratives of exclusion (Kohl and Fawcett 1995), which potentially can lead to racist narratives.

Accusations of racist implications of genetic research have been put forward (Blake 2020; Bürmeister 2021), and here again we witness the collision of different metalanguages, leading to a critique that at least in part misses the point. Booth replied to Blake's critique of hidden racism in some DNA papers:

> I, and I think many population geneticists, would argue that terms such as "population" and "ancestry" are not euphemisms for race, and do not represent attempts to sanitize racial groups. In the discussion of human genetic diversity, terms like "population" and "ancestry" represent a convenient way of talking about genetic structure … Genetic structure is defined by the genetic data and not by pre-existing population labels. (Booth 2020: 18)

Here we are at the root of some current misunderstandings, lost in translation from genetic to archaeological metalanguage: When a genetic population for convenience is translated into an archaeological culture, such as Yamnaya or Corded Ware, it implies to many archaeologists an implicit correspondence between genes, culture, and ethnic identity – not least when further translated into popular dissemination. Therefore, utmost care and explanation is demanded when translating genetic and archaeological metalanguage (Eisenmann et al. 2018). Consequently, neutral terms to characterize genetic admixture processes are now being employed when possible, such as steppe ancestry, Anatolian/farmer ancestry, western and eastern hunter-gatherer ancestry. Accordingly, a discussion about good practice for making interdisciplinary interpretations is mandatory, and for that, a historical perspective provides a useful background (Díaz-Andreu and Coltofean-Arizancu 2021).

Archaeology and Genetics: Toward a New Interdisciplinarity

I will summarize some commonalities reflected in the present debates between geneticists and archaeologists, most clearly expressed by Tim Flohr Sørensen (2017a and b), Alexandra Ion (2017), and Martin Furholt (2018), or between archaeologists and environmental scientists (Arponen et al. 2019a and 2019b; Kristiansen 2019). The recent debates also voice a widespread anxiety among archaeologists that science-based genetic interpretations are taking precedence over archaeological interpretations (Samida and Eggert 2013; Marila 2019).

The debate raises a legitimate concern over how to integrate the two types of evidence from science and archaeology in a unified interpretation respecting both fields. In the words of Tim Flohr Sørensen, "we need to consider the potential that a question, an observation, an object, a fact, are not synonymous concepts in science and in the humanities. Why else would we apply different methods and theoretical perspectives?" (Sørensen 2017a and 2017b). While this may be correct, at least in part, the problems of interdisciplinary interpretation are of a more complex nature. No method can have priority over another, as methods are inherent to a specific scientific tradition. But if Sørensen is correct, then also no interpretation of a specific set of data can have priority over an interpretation of another set of data if they are confined within different discourses. Consequently, historical-archaeological interpretations are not inherently more correct than genetic interpretations. However, only by combining the two will it be possible to reach a full explanation that takes all evidence into account. In addition, there exists no genuine archaeological theory about human societies; what is inherently archaeological, besides excavation, is its repertoire of methods to describe changes in material culture. However, interpretation of that evidence can only be carried out by comparison from the known to the unknown, that is through comparative analysis with ethnographically and historically documented societies. Archaeological theory is therefore based on shared, comparative theoretical models of human societies anchored in social and historical research traditions. So-called Middle Range Theory is an attempt to bridge the two – archaeological data and theory – in order to create a more robust middle ground, but it does not add up to a complete social theory (Arponen et al. 2019c).

Thus, archaeology and genetics share the methodological demands of analytical systematics, statistical significance, and testable procedures in their basic repertoire. However, that does not produce a final interpretation; it demands a wider context, including comparative knowledge of results from other disciplines. And that inevitably reduces the number of researchers who are capable and willing to provide that extra investment of labor in a new field where such interpretations for the foreseeable future will remain debatable. Until now the most productive way forward has been project teamwork, where archaeologists, geneticists, and researchers from other relevant disciplines such as environmental science, historical linguistics, and so on, work together, from formulating research goals through to final publication.

Therefore, the real challenge is how we balance evidence from different disciplines in interpretation. As there exists no methodological approach that is able to combine and statistically evaluate results from, say, environmental analysis, genetics, and archaeology against each other, the task is a difficult one. You may be able to document statistical correlations between such different types of evidence, as has been done recently (Racimo et al. 2020b), but there is a giant step from correlation to explanation and interpretation. We may well see complex modeling in the future that is able to handle the task of weighting qualitatively different types of data as to their relative impact in a historical process of change, but we are not there yet. It all comes down to the complexity of evidence that is anchored in different theoretical and methodological traditions and yet produces results that have an impact on the interpretation of other types of data.

In the end, final interpretation will have to be presented in the form of an interpretative narrative, where documentation is either found in a supplementary, most common in science journals, or simply based on previous research. Booth et al. 2020 provides an exemplary illustration of the first approach, raising new research questions and more particular interpretations, while Kristiansen et al. 2017 and Mittnik et al. 2019 are examples of the second approach, leading to more generalizing models. Therefore, we need to further develop the concept of interpretative narratives, which for a long time have been debated in the discipline of history (White 1987). But more recently, it has been suggested by Alexandra Ion as a way forward to integrate different strands of evidence from science and archaeology, calling it "archaeology as story-telling" (Ion 2017: 192). Perhaps it suffices for the moment to define such narratives as platforms for the formulation of new testable hypotheses. We may then perceive scientific practice as a layered process, moving from basic information through processes of proof/falsification toward increasingly wide-ranging interpretations and ending in an interpretative narrative (Figure 5) – this irrespective of whether we are talking about large geographical regions or narrow contextualized studies of single communities. The process remains the same, and results should in the end be compatible. If not, a new interpretation is needed, and the process starts all over again. To be proven wrong is the first step toward getting it right. In that sense, Colin Renfrew's contribution of integrating language and archaeology in new ways, even if now proven wrong, has been fundamental, since he propelled research forward with new speed and intensity. From a theoretical point of view, his interpretative models rejuvenated the interdisciplinary field by providing a strong interpretative narrative. We are now starting the process again.

The conclusion so far is that there is no easy fix to interdisciplinary collaboration and interpretation. It is demanding and sometimes fails to reach a balanced interpretation, and yet we cannot do without it. Some of the difficulties of interdisciplinary debate are also reflected in the present theoretical critique of the third science revolution, as exemplified by Booth (2019). One of the most common misunderstandings about genetic data is that a few samples cannot be statistically representative for human population history, which they in fact can (explained in Booth 2019). Thus, if you want to practice interdisciplinarity, it takes time and effort to understand the other side of the "Two Cultures" – the concept introduced by Snow in his classic paper (Snow 1959). Therefore, such a practice cannot be expected to be embraced by everyone. However, some critique is based on an ideological rejection of science rather than upon an understanding of the actual research results, much in the same vein as the early postprocessual critique (Martinon-Torres and Killick 2015). Without proper documentation, it describes interpretations based on science and archaeogenetics as being too "streamlined" and simplistic (Marila 2019), or it plays the "Kossinna Card" and reads ethnic, political messages into archaeological cultures and genetic populations that were most often never expressed nor intended

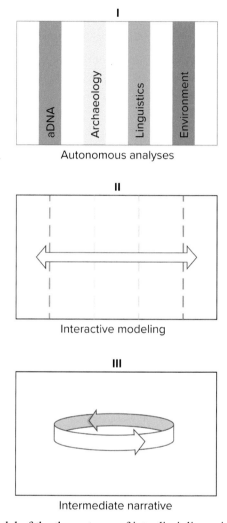

Figure 5 Model of the three stages of interdisciplinary interaction and collaboration. We can expect to see future developments especially for stage II. But the relative autonomy of each discipline in stage 1 should also be noted.

(Furholt 2018 with comments; Frieman and Hoffmann 2019 for a balanced discussion). Such attempts to dismiss or demonize archaeogenetic results are themselves simplistic, but some archaeogenetic papers admittedly invited this critique by exaggerating the archaeological and linguistic implications of their results in catchy, simplistic titles ("Massive Migration from the Steppe was a Source for Indo-European Languages in Europe"; "Origin of Minoans and Myceneans"; "Genetic Origin of Philistines"). Perhaps collisions of the "Two Cultures" are to be expected in a period of transition. However, interpretation, whether based on humanities or sciences, proceeds in a process of trial and error. The problem is first to agree what is erroneous and what is not within each discipline, and then to distinguish between genetic and cultural interpretations through a better understanding of their metalanguage. Here, there is still a gulf of mutual misunderstandings to be overcome (Lalueza-Fox 2013; Liden and Eriksson 2013).

2 Theoretical and Methodological Framework

The third science revolution, like all scientific revolutions (Kuhn 1962), is both disruptive and productive. Disruptive in the sense that it undermines many held theoretical beliefs and exposes our inability to correctly interpret the archaeological evidence when it comes to migrations and material culture. Productive in the sense that it has invited renewed attempts to retheorize migrations, as well as the role of material culture, even if such an endeavor is still in its infancy.

The Challenge in Front of Us: Retheorizing Genetic and Cultural Change

Therefore, the challenge in front of us is to develop better theoretical frameworks for understanding the relationship between genetic and cultural change, and in addition to develop better frameworks for the collaboration between archaeology and genetics. This has been pointed out in several recent debate papers (Callaway 2018; Eisenmann et al. 2018; Furholt 2017; Ion 2017; Kristiansen 2019; Sørensen 2017a). A theoretical reorientation should aim at combining the micro- and the macroperspective, things, humans and societies, as genetics and strontium analysis allows this kind of resolution (Frei et al. 2015 and 2017; Kristiansen et al. 2017). However, rather than having mystifying things as agents, I wish to reintroduce humans, their social institutions, technologies, and cultural environments as driving or constraining factors. A materialist Marxist perspective allows us to understand that things are not what humans envision them to be. This refers to Marx's concept of fetishism. A fetish is an object believed to have supernatural powers. Marx coined the concept to characterize money and markets in early capitalism as fetishism, since liberal economists ascribed to them an inherent supernatural or self-regulating power, which according to Marx was demonstratively derived from human actions based on the relationship between production, distribution, and consumption (Marx 1953 and 1974: introduction). By not including the value of labor in the equation, profits seemed magically to arise from market demands and price differences rather than from labor (Marx 1953; 1974). Marx spent much of his later life in a partly failed attempt to demonstrate scientifically how this economic system worked, in order to unfold its laws (Liedman 2018). The point I wish to make here is that, in much the same way, we can attribute fetishism to modern thing theory and posthuman theories (Hornborg 2016). According to Hornborg, fetishism in this wider definition represents a false attribution of power, "the displacement of responsibility – to objects within networks of social relations where the political agency of humans is not apparent" (2016: 172).

Thus, when critically compared with Marxist materialism, the so- called "New Materialism" in archaeology (Witmore 2014), anthropology, and cultural theory (Coole and Frost 2010) is rather a nonhuman-based pseudomaterialism, trapped in fetishism, and therefore unable to explain historical processes. In *Global Magic*, Hornborg (2016: 7) referred to this phenomenon as the abandonment of relationism, and thus the abandonment of human power and responsibility, effectively leaving explanations of global environmental problems to natural science. The third science revolution allows the reintroduction of a new interdisciplinary social, science-based theory of history and human agency based on the material conditions of life.

Basic to such a reinvigoration of social theory is an understanding of the primary role of institutions in organizing society and its power relations (Bondarenko et al. 2020; archaeological application in Kristiansen and Larsson 2005: chapter 1.2). Material culture and language make institutions possible; they provide social identity and behavioral norms to groups; they provide a blueprint for action. Thus, by institutionalizing technology and economy through material culture imbued with symbolic power (fetishism), social and religious networks organize production/distribution and allow the manipulation of power. In Figure 6, I have summarized these relationships. All relations originate in the social organization of the political economy through the manipulation of things, infusing them with symbolic power, well explained by Alfred Gell (1998), thereby transferring power over things through prestige goods and sacred objects to power over people. This basic dynamic has been at work from the beginning of modern humans in the Paleolithic to the Industrial Age. Therefore, we can apply a general Marxist materialist theory for all human history since the Paleolithic, one that encapsulates the human condition from the individual to emerging World Systems (Figure 7).

Following from this, political economies and their modes of production (Kristiansen and Earle 2022) are always to be understood as exploitative, whether of environments or humans, and thus deeply embedded in contested social relationships (Figure 7). Modes of production specify how individuals access the economy to mobilize revenues to support and institutionalize political power. Institutions thus organize production, circulation, and consumption,

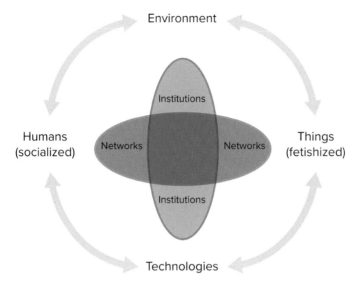

Figure 6 Model of the basic organizing categories of society and their dynamics. It shows how networks and institutions integrate social and material worlds, environments, and technologies

which form relations of production. A crucial theoretical concern is to describe how surplus labor and surplus wealth are generated and distributed, as this entails the dynamics behind both migratory processes and processes of hierarchization. They are dialectically related, as we shall demonstrate, and unfold according to a set of recurring circumstances through prehistory. With this as my starting point, I shall look more closely into the nature of culture and society, and after that migrations, their organization and driving forces. However, before doing that I wish to situate my theoretical approach within the wider context of competing discourses and ontologies and their role in understanding and explaining the past.

Complementary or Colliding Ontologies? Ways of Addressing the Complexity of Past and Present Societies

I wish to propose that no single theoretical discourse or ontology is able to account for and explain the complexity of either past or present societies. The main strength of Marxist materialist and processual theories are their ability to address and explain the social and economic forces of history and the role of social institutions. Social and economic regularities and transformations are the main objectives. The focus is on "real" objective forces of history and a wish to unmask subjective illusions of ritual and religion as proper explanations (see my discussion of "fetishism" in the previous section). Such theories belong in

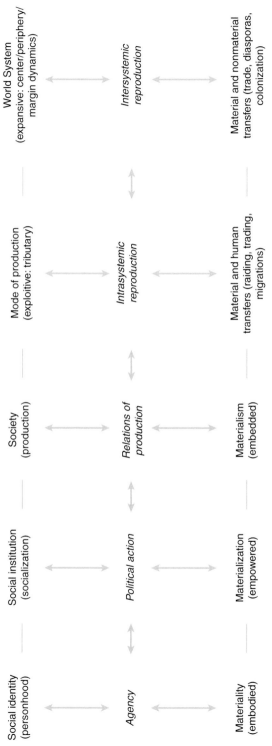

Figure 7 Conceptual model of forces of power in human societies that integrates micro- and macrodynamics

a long academic tradition that puts humans and society at center stage. In some opposition to this, we find posthumanistic and phenomenological ontologies, which attempt to understand the world in itself, abandoning a modern objectivist approach with humans at center stage in favor of a situated self-understanding of past and present ontologies and cosmologies, putting humans, animals, and things on equal terms. They are part of a long academic tradition of hermeneutic understanding and of the phenomenological experience of "Being" there (Tilley 1994), with an attempt to avoid binary perceptions of the world (Crellin and Harris 2020). Both traditions have been used and misused by totalitarian regimes in ideologically tainted versions (communism and fascism), which underlines the role of humanities in the present to understand and shape the world. This political, ideological connection goes some way to explain their cyclical history of dominance since Enlightenment, as shown in Figure 3.

Right now, we are witnessing a debate between humanist/materialist and posthumanist ontologies (Díaz de Liaño and Fernández-Götz 2021). Such attempts are part of the ongoing fight for theoretical supremacy, which, however, tends to obscure the complexity of both present and past societies. The point I wish to make, or rather reiterate, is that no single ontology can fully grasp and explain human existence. It can reveal important aspects but can never stand alone. Understanding the complexity of prehistoric societies demands the application of complex and theoretically informed interpretations. Different ontologies may coexist, even if one ontology may be the dominant one. Thus, different subsistence economies such as foragers and farmers employ different ontologies. In ethnographic case studies from Borneo (Nikolaisen 1976), it has been shown that farmers consider the natural forest as dangerous, to be avoided. Here live the foragers, for whom the forest is inhabited by spirits and is their habitat. They have a taboo against felling trees, while farmers cut down the forest to create fields for cultivation. The farmers' habitat is the cultivated, encultured landscape, and they consider themselves more civilized than the foragers, with whom they conduct restricted trade for forest products, but otherwise they do not intermix. In short, these two groups apply opposite cosmologies/ontologies and occupy different habitats. With farming, a more dual or binary perception of nature/culture is introduced (Barrett 2019), and this is further developed in pastoral economies in the application of strict gender divisions in burial rituals and social life (Kristiansen et al. 2017; Furholt 2019), which is continued during the Bronze Age. However, central aspects of an undivided, naturalized ontology are retained in religion, where the forces of animals and nature (the sun and moon) are mobilized, a trend that continues during the Iron Age, where we witness a world of hybrid animal/human transformations (Hedeager 2010; Kaliff and Oestigaard 2021).

It is therefore fully justified to apply a posthumanistic ontology in the study of the past, because it entails important insights. A more recent example is Joakim Goldhahn's book *Birds in the Bronze Age* (Goldhahn 2019), which springs from an ontological strand of understanding human–animal relationships in new, nonhuman ways (Oma and Goldhahn 2020). Even if Goldhahn, as expected, criticizes previous theoretical interpretations as being incomplete (which remains universally true of all interpretations), his work nonetheless profits from the Bronze Age being so well studied and well explained, so that he can add a new interpretative layer with an enhanced understanding of Bronze Age *Worldings*, to use one of his favorite phrases. These new insights may in turn lead to revised interpretations of previous models (Kveiborg 2018 and 2020). In the present Element, I consciously apply a materialist "Marxist" ontology of human-based social institutions as the more productive for my purpose, namely to understand and explain processes of social, cultural, and genetic changes through later prehistory. Once such a foundation is established, I am sure other ontologies can be applied successfully, even if some would argue they should already form part of our understanding of archaeogenetics (Crellin and Harris 2020). Therefore, both ontologies, human and nonhuman-based, are needed to grasp the full complexity of past societies (Gosden 1999: part II). I have summarized their complementary roles in Figure 8.

Humans, Culture, and Society

One of the most enduring debates in archaeology is about how material culture relates to various forms of identities in the past, first and foremost the concept of culture, and related to that the concept of ethnicity (Roberts and Vander Linden 2011; Curta 2014). It may therefore be helpful to provide first a brief history of the debate and then to attempt a definition of both culture and ethnicity. In a recent overview, Roberts and Vander Linden stated that "the long-term persistence over time and space of archaeological cultures is related to the fact that they represent patterns in the archaeological record whose significance, if any, remains obscure to archaeologists" (Roberts and Vander Linden 2011: 8). This apparent paradox is due to the fact that culture has both an instrumental and an interpretative side. I stated this in my contribution to the volume in the following way:

> The concept of culture has been employed in two different ways in archaeology: from the 1860s to 1960s, culture was predominantly used in an instrumental way, as a means to classify the past in time and space. Typology was the method. As there existed no theory as to the meaning of culture, early attempts to equate culture and people were flawed, as we know. (Kristiansen 2011: 201)

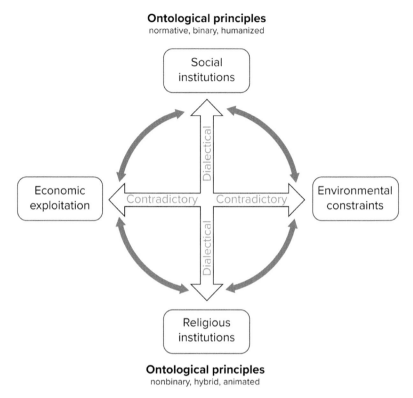

Figure 8 Model of the theoretical complementarity of two dominant ontologies

Culture is thus a covering concept, like diffusion, whose meaning depends on interpretation and ultimately upon the methodological classification of culture. What aspects of culture are classified – pots, prestige goods, or burial rituals? Each material category and context refers back to different institutions in society and thus demands a theoretical framework that situates material culture in its social and institutional context (Kristiansen and Larsson 2005: figure 2). The so-called "rise and fall" of the concept of culture is thus mainly related to disputes over its interpretative status, which I shall briefly discuss, with a nod to its methodological development as well.

The Concept of Culture: Practical Use versus Historical Interpretation

The concept of culture as a methodological strategy of typological classification has remained one of the buildings blocks of archaeology since Hans Hildebrandt and especially Oscar Montelius developed the method of typology during the later nineteenth century (Baudou 2012). Montelius demonstrated its feasibility in the first major study of the Nordic Bronze Age in 1885 and later applied the method to classify the Bronze Age cultures of Europe and the Near East in 1903. By that time, the method had been universally adopted as the basic tool of classification of archaeological material culture from the Paleolithic to the Iron Age. Oscar Montelius himself, however, did not take the step from classification to interpretation in his academic works, but he did so in a popular work on "the immigration of our forefathers to the North," which appeared in 1884 in Swedish (Baudou 2005). This work was translated into German in 1888, and it inspired Gustaf Kossinna to write his famous paper on "Die vorgeschichtliche Ausbreitung der Germanen in Deutschland" (1896).[3] In this paper, he made the bold statement that one could equate an archaeological culture with a people, understood as an ethnic group. Based on his own academic background as a philologist with a good knowledge of classical and linguistic sources, and their mentioning of ethnic groups in the Iron Age, he proceeded to combine the two – archaeological cultures and historically known ethnic groups. He then made a follow-up statement, that if one could trace historically known groups back in time through the persistence of sharply defined archaeological cultures, it implied also ethnic persistence. This had previously been formulated by Montelius as a possibility, not as a statement. Likewise, if an archaeological culture could be demonstrated to expand, it reflected a migration or expansion of that group. While Montelius is at pains in his work to stress that archaeological circumstances *can* offer us information about a migration, not that it must provide a positive or negative response, as stated in Evert Baudou's analysis (Baudou 2005: 125–6), Gustaf Kossinna removed such methodological reservations to produce a compelling historical narrative of the Germanic people. Prehistory could suddenly be used to trace back in time the origin and expansion of present-day peoples, as summarized in his famous book from 1911 (Kossinna 1911).

Quite evidently, such long-term persistence of ethnic groups invited politicization, not least in a climate of rising nationalism, even if there was rarely, if ever, congruence between present-day nation states and archaeological cultures, and even if what constituted cultural continuity remained a matter of debate (Jacob-Friesen 1928; Eggers 1959). In the nondemocratic political regimes of Europe

---

[3] Gustaf Kossinna's admiration of Oscar Montelius shines through in a letter to him: "I have endeavoured mainly to follow in the footsteps of the Scandinavian masters, amongst whom you have always incontestably occupied the highest rank. Your masterly ingenuity revealed to me ten years ago ('Tidsbestämning') the methodological stringency that must prevail even in pre-historic studies and made me a lasting disciple of this science. Your works, of which I own several of those that have been published separately (such as 'Tidsbestämning,' 'Kultur Schwedens,' 'Temps préhistorique en Suede'), have been my lodestar, as have your innumerable journal articles to perhaps an even greater extent" (from Schwerin von Krosigk 1982: 168).

before and after the Second World War, widespread archaeological distributions exceeding present-day nation states were sometimes used to seek legitimization of political and military expansion of either so-called Germanic or Slavonic tribal territories (Kristiansen 1993: figure 4; Díaz-Andreu and Champion 1996).

Such far-reaching historical interpretations therefore became hotly debated but nonetheless also widely applied in European archaeology, often implicitly (Veit 1989; Heyd 2017). They had a parallel in the ethnographic and ethnological theories of the Vienna School about cultural circles (*Kulturkreislehre*) (Rebay- Salisbury 2011), and to some extent also in the work of the Boas School in the USA (Boas 1911), which was a return to the importance and meaning of the particular and its cultural context. If that sounds familiar, it is because Ian Hodder and postprocessualism took inspiration from Boas when they redefined culture in the 1980s as "meaningfully constituted" and historically contextualized. In short, they wanted to revive material culture as an interpretative tool (Hodder 1982a, 1982b, 1982c). However, this again was a reaction against two competing approaches toward material culture exemplified in the works of David Clarke and Colin Renfrew.

The Clarke–Renfrew–Hodder–Shennan Debate

Despite critical debates and attempts to eradicate culture as a meaningful theoretical concept, the classification of material culture has remained an independent, instrumental exercise in European archaeology up until the present, for purposes of ordering. It reached a methodological climax in David Clarke's famous *Analytical Archaeology* from 1968, where quantification and modeling were added to empower the analytical approach of classification. It allowed a fine-grained and stepwise exposition of different layers of cultural patterning, from local and regional culture groups with geographical distributions from 20 to 200 to 750 miles (Clarke 1968: figure 58) to global technocomplexes with geographical distributions from 700 to 3,000 miles (Clarke 1968, chapter 8, page 331). Clarke employed the concept of "polythetic" traits as constituting elements of culture (Clarke 1968: table II, page 299), yet without abandoning culture as a definable, multilayered spatial phenomenon. This new platform was subsequently employed by Ian Hodder to redefine and reinterpret spatial pattering (Hodder and Orton 1976; Hodder 1978).

In opposition to this approach, Colin Renfrew denounced the concept of culture in archaeology, which he wanted to replace with polities, governed by theoretically informed, testable generalizations (Renfrew 1977). In short, he wanted to put theory before method and consequently define the material attributes needed to test a theory, rather than starting with classification and then trying to make sense of it. His approach questioned the reality of prehistoric cultures as constructs of the present, an old debate in American archaeology. A critical reanalysis done by Stephen Shennan of the Bell Beaker culture demonstrated it to be nonhomogenous and constituted by different spatial distributions, depending on type of material analyzed (Shennan 1978). Such results were rather in accordance with David Clarke's polythetic approach to culture as multilayered, and to be expected. Yet, it demanded a more theoretically informed approach on how to interpret this variation. In this situation, Ian Hodder redefined culture as meaningfully constituted with a clear symbolic role in organizing society. Inspired by the work of David Clarke (1968), he accepted the historical reality of culture and its role in demarcating various forms of identities, past and present, but added to it a comparative theoretical framework as to the symbolic meaning of culture (Hodder 1982b and 1982c). He was also inspired by the ethnographic work of Fredrik Barth on the role of ethnicity in demarcating borders of identity and power (Barth 1969). His tentative hypotheses from 1978 were subsequently tested in ethnographic fieldwork published in *Symbols in Action* in 1982 (Hodder 1982b).

Thus, by employing a comparative ethnographic approach to the use and meaning of material culture, Hodder provided a new theoretical framework for revitalizing the concept of culture, which, however, never really gained momentum, perhaps except in his own works (Hodder 1982a, 1982b, 1982c, and 1990), and in some edited books (Hodder 1982a; Shennan 1989). His later work on entanglement did not relate to the concept of culture and ethnicity, but rather to understanding the multitude of human–thing relations (Hodder 2016), which represents another discourse.

An example of the continued inspiration from David Clarke is to be found in the role played by cultural transmission in recent evolutionary studies of material culture, as represented in the works of Stephen Shennan and others (Mace et al. 2005). It represents a return to a more processual archaeology, coupled to concepts from biological evolution, and along with that quantification and modeling of cultural regularities. Stephen Shannan summarized the various approaches under the umbrella of "Darwinian archaeology" (Shennan 2002) and positioned his approach in opposition to some of the more extreme relativist approaches in postprocessual archaeology, linked to historical contingency, agency, and developments in phenomenological approaches that abandoned quantification and historical regularities (discussion in Kristiansen 2004). While I was initially skeptical about the use of biological evolutionary theory to explain cultural transmission without relating it to social institutions (Kristiansen 2004), there is no doubt that Darwinian archaeology in its broader sense has reignited and invigorated the methodological field in archaeology, with new approaches to how to analyze and model not only material culture but more generally various types of big data, from C-14 dates to ecological, environmental, and economic data. Theoretical and mathematical models are increasingly able to combine contingency and agency with evolutionary and historical regularities, as suggested more the twenty years ago (Gould 1999; Bintliff 1999; Kristiansen 2004: figure 5). Today the "Great Divide" between science-based modeling and humanistic particularism and agency is increasingly being bridged (Racimo et al. 2020a, 2020b), also exemplified in the way Ian Hodder applied evolutionary theory to his entanglement theory (Hodder 2016: chapter 2). Martin Furholt has also in several recent studies employed David Clarke's concept of culture as polythetic in an attempt to explain the complexity of third-millennium migrations and their later consolidation (Furholt 2019 and 2020). It shows that lines of intellectual and theoretical history are still reverberating in the present.

In conclusion, theoretical and interpretative developments from the 1980s into the early 2000s centered on the role of culture as a transmitter of symbolic meaning, rather avoiding its role in creating ethnic identity. Thus, there remained widespread resistance to entering the politically tainted field of ethnic interpretation, even if attempts have been made (Chrisomalis and Trigger 2003; Fernández-Götz 2013; Fernández-Götz and Ruiz Zapatero 2011; Jones 1997; Reher and Fernández-Götz 2015), especially in the Mediterranean where written sources can often be employed (Cifani and Stoddart 2012; Hall 1997 and 2002; McInerney 2014, Renfrew 1998). In many ways, it represents a lost opportunity to revitalize archaeological cultural distributions in a dialogue with ethnographic and historical research on ethnicity. However, developments in Darwinian theory on material culture may also serve as inspiration to define robust material patterns of transmission and divergence. In my work with Thomas Larsson, we added the concept of social institutions to the interpretation of culture in order to integrate the symbolic and the social field into a single theoretical framework (Kristiansen and Larsson 2005: chapter 1). I shall now discuss this approach, as it represents a way out of the interpretative stalemate of culture, the role of ethnicity, and other forms of identity.

Culture and the Meaning of Social Institutions: Burials and Households

Social institutions are the building blocks of society, from the Palaeolithic to the present. In short, they constitute the way modern humans employ culture as a symbolic field to define roles and rules for social, ritual, and economic behavior (Runciman 2001; Bondarenko et al. 2020; Hodder 2016). The task then becomes to identify those material structures and contexts that define various types of institutions. Such an approach recombines theoretical and methodological elements from Clarke, Hodder, and Renfrew. It allows the integration of polities and institutions with their spatial coverage (Kristiansen and Larsson 2005: figure 2). To begin, we need to recognize the dialectic relation between norm and variability in material culture. Difference and sameness are both properties of cultural norms – one cannot perceive difference without a norm for sameness. Here, we are at the heart of what constitutes the relation between identities of various forms, including ethnic identity, and the role of material culture in defining these very same identities through variation. As a next step, one has to relate this material variation to an institution, whether a specific social group or a religious or political elite. Without that identification, we cannot proceed, since it is institutions that constitute and provide identity to a group. However, certain symbolic markers can sometimes have a primary role in defining a specific institution, such as the flange-hilted sword of the Bronze Age warrior, which transcends different cultural groups in Europe and creates its own transcultural identity. It reminds us that some institutions transcend traditional cultural borders, and that social and institutional identities can be multilayered and multifunctional (Kristiansen and Larsson 2005: figure 3). A warrior may both belong to a local chiefly retinue and household and at the same time be part of a larger transcultural brotherhood of a warrior sodality. Other symbolic markers are rather more regional and ethnic, such as the Nordic full-hilted sword, which represents an institution of ritual leadership, while other symbolic markers may refer to a local identity, often reflected in specific types of ornaments or small-scale variations in pottery styles (Kristiansen and Larsson 2005: figure 168). Such institutional "reference symbols" are important to identify – they were referred to as "institutional facts" by Colin Renfrew (2000), and as "ethnic markers" by Manuel Fernández-Götz (2013). Each case demands its own contextual analysis and interpretation in order to define the relevant institutions and their symbolic references. In the following sections, such variation and its meaning will be demonstrated. Here, I shall discuss the significance of some basic institutions, such as burial rituals and households.

The Transformative Role of Burial Rituals

Some social institutions are more fundamental than others, in the sense that they define basic social and ritual properties that cannot be easily replaced or altered without changing the whole social and economic organization of society (its mode of production). Since rituals and religion sanctify social and economic order, burial rituals represent one of the most basic institutions in any society. The generational change of power that death represents sets in motion a series of processes linked to basic rules sustaining social continuity. They include rules of inheritance and the transmission of various forms of property to the next generation, and the renewal of social and political obligations. Therefore, a funeral becomes a social gathering of kin and alliance partners to show their respect towards the deceased person, who will now take their place among the ancestors and from there exercise another form of power to uphold the lineage. However, this also becomes an occasion for the kin of the deceased to renew alliances and receive or pay debt and other forms of obligations of the deceased (Oestigaard and Goldhahn 2006).

Therefore, burial rituals reflect basic elements of social organization, even when they are absent. Thus, there can be no doubt that the collective ritual of megalithic burials tells a story of a more communal or clan-based organization of society than the single-grave burial ritual of Yamnaya and Corded Ware societies, where the ritual focus is on the individual as a social and ritual persona. I have previously described the significance of burial rituals for the identification of population movements:

> A strong relationship exists between burial ritual and social and religious institutions, because a burial is the institutionalized occasion for the transmission of property and power, and the renewal of social and economic ties (Oestigaard and Goldhahn 2006). A radical change in burial rites therefore signals a similar change in beliefs and institutions. If such a change occurs rapidly without transition it signals a transformation of society, often under strong external influence, possibly a migration (to be supported also by settlement change and economic change). This does not rule out the effects of internal contradictions, which, however, often go hand in hand with external forces of change. (Kristiansen et al. 2017)

The shared institution of the single-burial ritual of Yamnaya and Corded Ware societies was later documented by Martin Furholt in an important paper that also added interesting regional variations (Furholt 2019: figures 2 and 3). The institution of the single-burial ritual thus conformed well with the genetic evidence and added regional variations that reflected the cultural transformations from Yamnaya to Corded Ware and later inside Corded Ware (Figure 9).

The Transformation of Household Organization

Another basic institution in all prehistoric societies is that of the household and its organization (Madella et al. 2013). Ian Hodder expressed the symbolic significance of the household to Neolithic society in the term "domus" and its development towards "agrios" (Hodder 1990, chapters 3–4). Thus, after the Mesolithic period, European prehistoric societies were formed by two distinct social and economic traditions linked to colonizing migrations: from 6000 BC onward that of Anatolian farming communities and after 3000 BC that of steppe

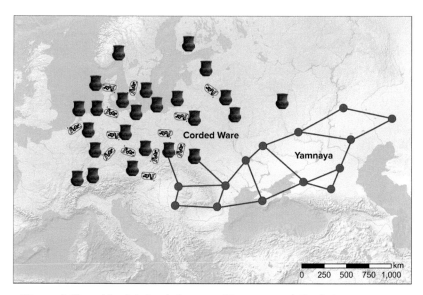

Figure 9 Shared burial rituals between Yamnaya and Corded Ware groups
(redrawn from from Furholt 2019 and 2021)

pastoral groups. Their admixture formed the specific social and cultural traditions that after 2000 BC shaped European Bronze and Iron Age societies. We
therefore need to understand the basic differences and similarities between
these two "Great Traditions," in the terminology of Robert Redfield and Knut
Odner (Odner 2000: chapter 2).

The farming societies that originated in Anatolia represented a Near Eastern
tradition of community-based tell settlements that gradually underwent social
and economic adaptations during their expansion first into the Mediterranean
and Balkans (Chapman 2020), and later into central Europe and beyond
(Shennan 2018). I have modeled the different social and economic dynamics
of these two Great Traditions (Figures 10a and 10b). We observe a gradual
separation of house and burial. In Anatolia and the Near East, houses became
burial places of the household leaders over time, as they were buried under the
floor (Hodder 1990: figure 1.2). When the Linearbandkeramik (LBK) split off
from Balkan/Carpathian tell communities to continue colonization of the central European temperate zone (Figure 11), large longhouses of several
(extended) family groups replaced communal tell village life, and burials
subsequently moved outside the house. Other groups expanded toward
Ukraine, forming large-scale agglomerations of highly organized megasettlements, as in the developed phase of the Tripolje culture in Ukraine (Müller et al.
2016).

(a)

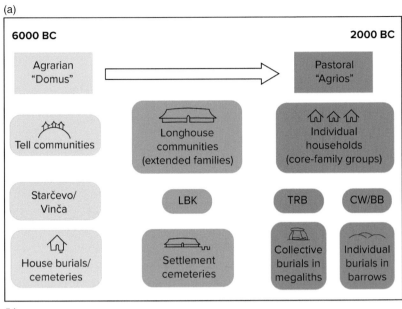

(b)

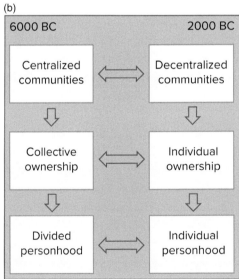

Figure 10a and b Model of agrarian and pastoral traditions in later European prehistory, leading to different institutions of marriage and kinship systems, and subsequently also to different processes of hierarchization

Both the LBK and the Tripolje megasettlements represent an agrarian-based, labor-intensive form of farming, where much labor was needed during some periods of the year, meaning that single households were too small to

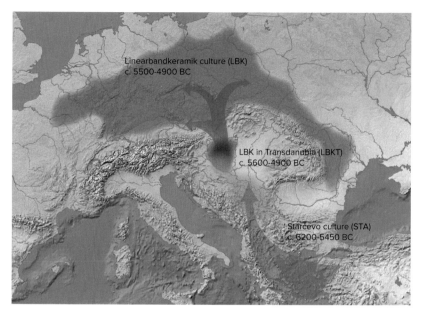

Figure 11 Map of the expansion of Neolithic economies and the change from tell societies to longhouse societies (redrawn from Szécsényi-Nagy et al. 2015)

survive on their own. One can therefore discuss what constituted a household in such a community-based settlement organization. One should rather see various conglomerates of household constellations as forming suprahouseholds inside the larger community. By suprahousehold, I imply that they are large enough to form a functioning unit that can reproduce itself socially and economically if needed, which again was a precondition for colonizing new landscapes during the Neolithic period.

When these larger tell-based settlements centered on intensive farming reached the temperate forested zone in Hungary, they split up into smaller settlements where suprahouseholds were confined within a new type of timber-built longhouse for several family groups (Bánffy 2006 and 2019). It represented an adaptation to a wetter and colder climate and to soils of less productivity perhaps than Ukraine's black soils and those of the Balkans. Called "house societies," using a term from Levi-Strauss (Bickle et al. 2016), these new types of households retained elements of tell organization but scaled down and adapted to a new climate and landscape. The basic suprahousehold could now be contained within a longhouse, even if such longhouses tended to cluster together and form demographically stronger settlement units with a larger potential both to clear new land and also to defend themselves.

This separation is completed during the continued geographical and temporal farming expansion towards western and northern Europe after 4000 BC, when the ideological concept of the longhouse is transformed to create a new monumental burial ritual of long barrows, later to become large megaliths. What we witness here is a gradual transformation of the institution of the household from containing both living and dead to a separation of the two. It reflects a new economic strategy of smaller movable households, where the burial monument takes over the central role of defining the continuity of the lineage and its control of land, in conjunction with the new institution of large ritual enclosures serving supralocal functions (Hodder 1990: figure 6.7). Yet, a communal ideology is maintained in the burial ritual even if it is disappearing in settlement organization.

The full ritual consequence of this economic and social transformation is seen in the pastoral economy of Yamnaya and later Corded Ware groups, where the individual is now at the ritual center stage in small family barrows and settlements are movable. Bronze Age households of individual farmsteads dominated throughout most of temperate Europe after 3000 BC. This represented the final result of a long-term development from early, more self-contained, centralized farming communities in larger settlements during the Neolithic toward a more decentralized society where political and economic control could be exercised over larger territories and therefore did not demand such concentrations of people in large settlements. Individual ownership of land and animals, rather than collective or communal ownership, was part of this historical transformation. In the Bronze Age, free land-owning farmers controlled individual farms, including cattle and grazing land (some probably shared), which allowed them to cut the sods of such grazing land for barrows for their chiefly ancestors, and also to use cattle skin and meat in burial rituals. In short, a household was more than an economic institution; it also provided surplus production to maintain a ritual economy, as well as a social and commercial economy where warrior retinues played an important role (Holst et al. 2013). A select group of free chiefly lineages maintained and controlled these vital institutions in society. They could be maintained through the principle of primogeniture, which in effect would send off surplus sons to make their own career, whether as warriors, colonizers, or just becoming labor.

Such different forms of household organization, linked to differences in social and economic organization as well as environmental differences, would produce different forms of burial traditions, and they would also be manifest in different forms of cultural and ethnic identities, which I shall now discuss.

From Cultural Identity to Ethnicity and Back

Critiques of Ethnicity

It remains an unexplored paradox that as soon as the archaeological record is supplemented by written sources, we find ethnic groups all over the place (Rankin 1987). The same is true of nearly all ethnographic research – human groups identify themselves in one way or another against other groups, and by name (Barth 1969; Hornborg and Hall 2011; Hornborg 2014). Even if some of those ethnic labels may sometimes have been employed for political purposes in ancient texts that characterize so-called barbarian societies and their geography (Rankin 1987; Dueck 2012), it is a historical fact that cultural and ethnic identities are basic to all human groups. Therefore, it remains a paradox that these concepts have been consciously avoided in most prehistoric research, in some opposition to the situation in ancient history and classical archaeology (McInerney 2014). Normally it is explained by reference to their political abuse in the past, the so-called "Kossinna" syndrome, a card that is often played when criticizing recent genetic research and its use of generally accepted cultural terms such as Yamnaya and Corded Ware culture (Heyd 2017; Furholt 2017). While such critique could be justified as a warning against simplistic interpretations of genetic admixture processes in some of the early papers, which applied rather wide-ranging interpretations (Haak et al. 2015), awareness of these problems was taken on board in subsequent works. In a paper on the Bell Beaker migrations from 2018, the use of cultural labels is properly cautioned in the supplementary text to the paper: "Beakers and associated artefacts do have strong similarities across western and central Europe, but there is also substantial variation, which has made many archaeologists uncomfortable with the term 'culture'" (Heyd et al. 2018). Noting that there are diverging interpretations of the Beaker phenomenon, the authors state: "By focusing on the genetic facts, we hope that archaeologists across the spectrum of opinions will perceive this study as a reliable presentation of the genetic findings and thus as a valuable reference for future debates."

Such cautions have either escaped most critics or are unconsciously forgotten. Perhaps an element of self-critique should be exercised. After all, we as prehistoric archaeologists neglected to develop a more advanced, and theoretically informed, understanding of archaeological cultures and their complexity, with some minority exceptions already discussed. Therefore, the repeated critique, especially by Martin Furholt, on the use of commonly accepted cultural labels, such as Corded Ware culture and Bell Beaker phenomenon/culture, in archaeogenetic studies, as representing a dangerous misrepresentation of prehistoric groups as homogenous entities and a return to a simplistic interpretative past, is mostly not justified when reading the papers he criticizes. And when he and others in addition play the "race card," we enter a dangerous ideological demonization of a whole field of research: "We archaeologists have found ourselves facing a veritable rollback of seemingly long-overcome notions of static cultures and a biologization of social identities, something that is clearly connected to the idea of races ... And this rollback is connected to the massive impact of ancient-DNA studies on archaeology" (Furholt 2020: 23–5). These sweeping generalizations lack precise documentation and merely assume that general cultural labels, rather than being descriptive, are interpretative and loaded with an implicit ethnic, even racist, meaning. This may indeed be the case in some popular communication of the results, and it is here that care should be exercised, as already discussed ("The Danger of Ideological Misrepresentation").

The whole issue of the meaning of genetic and cultural categories and their translation is indeed complex (Sykes et al. 2019). However, it should be recognized that critique of the use of cultural categories as potentially misleading by Furholt and others had the positive effect of turning attention to the problem, as seen in the paper by Eisenmann et al. (2018), and it has also inspired this section on the meaning and role culture and ethnicity. The following reflections are therefore a preliminary attempt to address this complex issue.

Defining Ethnicity

I wish to start with a definition of the rationale of ethnicity, which goes some way to explain how it is constructed and how it works. Sian Jones in her foundational book, *The Archaeology of Ethnicity*, discusses and exemplifies the "primordial imperative" – the fact that ethnic markers and symbols are linked to the cosmological origin of a group, a tribe, a city state, or whatever ethnic entity we are talking about (Jones 1997: 65). Therefore, control over myths of origin becomes essential, and such myths cannot be easily replaced. When they are replaced, this is nearly always linked to a conquest when a "stranger king" takes power and a new lineage with more powerful origins comes to dominate. Myths of origin and ethnic identities therefore employ a symbolic language that becomes a trademark or a banner shared by all. This is exemplified in studies of some historically well-attested migrations of Langobards and Goths, who throughout their movements maintained their myth of origin in Scandinavia, signified by an elite symbolism (Hedeager

2010; Veeramah 2018). Such origins can now also be attested genetically, which raises a series of new critical questions to be addressed later.

From this primordial definition of ethnicity, we learn that it is upheld by elites, whether a warrior elite, a royal dynasty, or simply a chiefly lineage. It is about the legitimization of power and its institutions, representing a symbolic and perhaps more peaceful (legitimizing) side of power, but it is also about how myth and material culture become entangled in creating a worldview and an identity (Hedeager 2010). In leads to another important observation about the nature of ethnicity – it defines borders between "us" and "them," signified through material culture and sometimes language. It does not mean that such borders cannot be crossed – they can, but it demands knowledge of the ways to do so. Thus, I am now turning to what has been termed the instrumental side of ethnicity (Jones 1997: 72). Or put more simply, how is ethnicity formed and maintained, and what does it do?

Cultural identities and ethnicities are always formed in relation to and some-times in opposition to other such identities (Barth 1969; Sahlins 2010). From this arises the theoretical paradox that, while cultures are seemingly autonomous and often studied as such, they are derived from larger "global" processes of inter-linked political economies, which fuel a process of identification with certain cultural and cosmological values and material expressions. They are part of a process of elite formation and elite control, in need of boundaries to exert its dominance by establishing a system of shared values. Over time, cultural identity may come to include other forms of identification; for example, language may lend to it a certain degree of relative autonomy. While nationalism may have taken on more sophisticated and penetrating means of identity formation during the late modern period, it is shaped by the very same processes that led to the emergence of regional identities in the Neolithic and Bronze Age. They need therefore to be studied with due respect to these larger historical processes.

From a methodological point of view, boundary formation of various forms can often be demonstrated in the archaeological record, which define "us" and "them." (Hodder 1978; Bürmeister and Müller-Schessel 2007). We may assume that complex societies produced more boundaries than less complex societies, internal as well as external. The definition of such boundaries in the archaeo-logical record, however, is only a first step. Next follows the theoretical interpretation of the social and economic processes leading to such divisions in the material record. If they carry any weight, it must be possible to link them to the formation and reproduction of institutions. While ethnicity undoubtedly played a central role in all human societies as part of a common origin and shared historical identity and tradition, the primordial imperative and its mater-ial expressions have been an underdeveloped field of study (but see Bürmeister and Müller-Schessel 2007; Furholt 2008; Fernández-Götz 2013). I propose that it is possible to delimit various forms of social and ultimately ethnic identities, through a careful analysis of the geographical distribution of social institutions of power and the symbolic meaning of their material culture (Kristiansen 2014; Roberts and Vander Linden 2011; Vandkilde 1999). By identifying the relevant institutional frameworks in the archaeological record, it is possible to delimit various types of identities, from local to global, that helped to uphold and reproduce these very same institutions over shorter or longer periods of time. Here I identify a number of social institutions and their material expressions.

Polities and Local Identities: Ethnic Groups and Political Boundaries

The nature of local groups as defined in historical texts and in the archaeological record corresponds most closely to what, in ethnographic research by Barth (1969) and others, are termed "ethnic groups." They are rather localized, and they represent the limits of political power, eventually under a single king or chief, alternating with periods of coexisting chiefs or confederations. The materialization of such ethnic polities can take many forms but is mostly constituted by an association between specific objects and groups of people that represent local power. I shall exemplify this with reference to the well- studied Tumulus culture of the Middle Bronze Age in Europe and some well-documented Iron Age groups in Iberia.

In south-central Europe, during the period 1600 to 1300 BC, small variations in the material culture of female ornaments and pottery help to identify local groups (Figure 12) and demarcate areas under the political power or authority of leading chiefly clans (Wiegel 1992–4; Wels-Weyrauch 1989 and 2011), much in the same way as coinage in later historic times would assert the economic control of local kings. The fact that female ornaments served this function suggests the importance of controlling marriage strategies inside the territory, as well as the important social position held by these women. Also, local pottery produced by women may show similar distributions (Nebelsick 2005; Przybyla 2009: figures 105–9), in contrast to commercially produced pottery of later periods. It is interesting to note that, although female ornaments and pottery are used to demarcate local boundaries of polities, they are rich in religious and cosmological symbols that were shared throughout the Bronze Age world (Müller-Karpe 2004). Women were thus bearers of two important messages: a shared world of Bronze Age cosmology and a localized world of the political/ ethnic group. Their increasing visibility through bodily adornment and dress (Stig Sørensen and Rebay-Salisbury 2007) corresponds to their rising social status in burial rituals and later in hoards, which was a global trend in the Late

Tell cultures

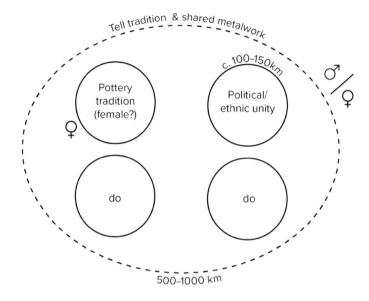

Tumulus cultures

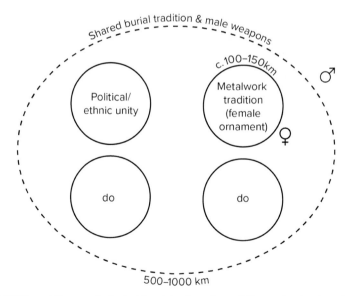

Figure 12 Different forms of ethnic identities based on different institutions in, respectively, central Europe (households and ritual hoarding), and northwestern Europe (burial rituals and burial wealth) during the Middle Bronze Age (redrawn from Kristiansen and Larsson 2005: figure 168)

Bronze Age, as demonstrated by Müller-Karpe (Müller-Karpe 1985; Kristiansen 1998: figure 32).

We are here encountering the social processes of consolidating political power through the exercise of control of women and their power of reproduction. It suggests that marriages between endogamous clans were now predominating, while exogamous marriages outside the territory were used to establish and maintain political alliances to allow the flow of goods and people between polities, including warriors and traders, forming confederacies (Gibson 2011). In this way, new forms of revenue from trade emerged that helped to consolidate political power. The control of women was reinforced in the subsequent period, when widow-burning often accompanied the burial of chiefly warriors with swords (Sperber 1999).

It has also been suggested that the formation of bounded political and ethnic territories coincides with a process of early state formation, as we know from early Iron Age protostates or complex chiefdoms throughout south and central Europe and the Mediterranean. Here, select forms of material culture are used to demarcate the limits of the polity, thereby also creating an internal identity in opposition to neighboring groups. One of the best-documented instances is the case of the Vettones in central Spain. Here, more than 400 bull statues, in combination with a specific form of pottery, demarcated the kingdom of the ethnic group (Alvarez-Sanchís 1999, 2002). It corresponded to the rise of fortified oppida and a ranked warrior society. From the early Iron Age onward, such ethnic polities were identified with a founding hero/king throughout Celtic Europe (Almagro-Gorbea and Lorrio 2011). Similar processes of territorial demarcation accompanied other early state formations in the Mediterranean (Cifani and Stoddart 2012). This use of material culture and rituals by select groups in the formation of early states has much in common with what we can observe from the Middle Bronze Age onward in Europe, with the exception of urbanization. Some of these processes also characterized the Neolithic period, which, however, remained more regionalized in terms of both trade and marriage alliances.

We should therefore allow for some variation in the use of material culture in the demarcation of political power. The Bronze Age examples suggest that we are dealing with processes of establishing some form of local territorial power, which we may even encounter in prestate ranked societies of the chiefdom type. It all comes down to definitions, but what remains important is that by the Bronze Age, but probably starting in the Neolithic, we see new forms of ranked political power that implied some form of control over producers and the formation of long-distance political alliances to ensure safe travels for traders, warriors, and other groups of people. This would most certainly also have implications for the diversification of language as well as borrowing (Iversen and Kroonen 2017).

We should consequently envisage the parallel existence of overlaying or coexisting forms of ethnic identification – from a local tribe or chiefdom to larger regional identities, in much the same way as a Greek city state would have a political and ethnic territory (Hall 1997, 2002) and yet be part of the larger entity of a Greek cultural koine of material culture, language, and ethnic identity (Malkin 2014). We should also be prepared to distinguish between ethnicity and other forms of cultural identity, which demands a contextualized study of the different forms of variability, and how these variations relate to different types of social institutions. Traders and warriors may exhibit one form of identity and social relatedness, while potters may produce another form. If potters are women and warriors are male, we may be able to establish gendered patterns of mobility and relate those patterns to the social institutions that produced them (Figure 12). This leads on to a discussion of how kinship institutions relate to ethnicity and ultimately to genetics and culture.

Principles of Kinship: Neolithic versus Bronze Age Kinship Institutions

Defining Kinship

I shall now discuss how different biological mating patterns from well-studied burial contexts with due caution can be translated into principles of social kinship. Genetics, in combination with strontium isotopes, makes it possible to discuss the other more critical aspect of the primordial imperative: what is the relation – if any – between ethnic origins and blood ties, and what is the role of kinship in maintaining or changing such relationships? And how do we define kinship in relevant prehistoric terms?

Kinship institutions and their rules of marriage, inheritance, fosterage, adoption, and so on represented the daily conduct of life within the tens of thousands of households that increasingly covered Europe during the Neolithic and later on during the Bronze Age. They are therefore fundamental to our understanding of the dynamics of social and economic reproduction in time and space. One of the most common principles of marriage in the anthropological literature is the matrilateral mother's brother's daughter cross-cousin marriage, or alternatively the patrilateral father's sister's daugh-ter. It represents an interpersonal way to create alliances between lineages (Sahlins 1968: chapter 4). Thus, traditional marriage is not strictly personal but rather a marriage of families. In the words of Marshall Sahlins, "kinship is a fundamental ground of peaceful human discourse. The wide extension of kinship idioms, relations, and groups in tribal societies represents another way to seek peace" (Sahlins 1968: 10).

However, to unravel marriage and kinship relations demands in-depth analyses of local community cemeteries, megaliths, or groups of barrows. As kinship institutions are integrated into larger networks, we may further assume that such case studies are valid for a region corresponding to the geographical origin of the analyzed individuals. Even if that provides some ground for generalization, we need many more in-depth local studies to provide larger spatial and temporal coverage than we have today, as we may assume that such institutions alter over time and may also display geographical variation. However, we already have at our disposal a number of mobility studies that have revealed basic principles of marriage and kinship institutions in later European prehistory from well-studied megaliths, barrows, and cemeteries (Fowler et al. 2021; Mittnik et al. 2019; Sjögren et al. 2021; Žegarac et al. 2021). Therefore, archaeology is, for the first time in its more-than-150-year history, in a position to contribute fresh data to the evolution of kinship systems, which may provide much-needed historical depth to the vast literature on ethnographic kinship studies. But it will demand active comparative research into various types of kinship systems. The literature on kinship systems is vast, and archaeology is yet to take on board a deeper understanding of how to apply kinship and marriage systems in prehistory (Johnson and Paul 2016). I adhere to a research tradition that considers marriage and kinship patterns as closely related to the political and economic organization of society, and thus to the reproduction of power structures (Friedman 1975; Gailey 1987; Levi-Strauss 1969). Even if there exist strong normative traditions, such practices are always negotiable and may thus change over time. Mary Helms demonstrates in her book *Access to Origins* how kinship strategies and ancestors can be used to make claim to origins and thus enable hierarchies (Helms 1998).

Kinship institutions can therefore be defined as social "ideal types" in the sense that their strict and normative rules are to be considered as guiding principles (Figure 13). However, in real life there are often deviations, where you bend the rules and invent relations or social ancestries to adapt to the rules. The anthropological literature is rife with such examples. However, since kinship and power relations are intrinsically interlinked, and since power relations may change over time, we should expect to see changes in principles of mating patterns defining new rules of kinship. Such changes can be introduced from the outside through migration, but they can also result from gradual adaptations to new conditions.

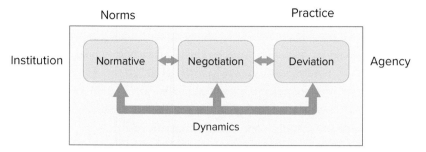

Figure 13 Dynamics of the institution of kinship

Neolithic and Copper Age Kinship Institutions

The nature of Neolithic kinship still defies proper definition. From the first strontium studies of LBK groups, it could be demonstrated that women were more mobile than men, therefore suggesting a form of exogamy among these colonizing family groups (Price et al. 2001). Later, more extensive strontium analyses of several hundred individuals (Bentley et al. 2012, also Bickle et al. 2016 for household differentiation) suggested a division into clans at cemeteries, and strontium analyses indicated viripatrilocal residence, but with differences between clans in their mobility patterns (Strien 2017). Marriage, however, seems to have taken place between the clans. These results were supported by a genetic study of LBK that concluded that "our results also reveal contrasting patterns for male and female genetic diversity in the European Neolithic, suggesting a system of patrilineal descent and patrilocal residential rules among the early farmers" (Szécsényi-Nagy et al. 2015; Furtwängler et al. 2020). Finally, a recent study of a Late Neolithic mass burials of fifteen men, women, and children from the Globular Amphora culture in Poland showed that they represented a large, extended family group based on patrilineal kinship. Four nuclear families were represented, mostly mothers and their children. Some siblings had different mothers, either suggesting serial marriage or polygamy. Their mothers, however, were probably also related to each other (Schroeder et al. 2019).

For the megalithic culture of northwestern Europe, a detailed study of strontium isotopes from a west Swedish passage grave from around 3000 BC revealed little difference in mobility between sexes, even if mobility was relatively high at around 20 percent (Sjögren et al. 2009). A study of twenty-four individuals from five megaliths, from Ireland, Orkney, Scotland, and Gotland (Sanchez-Quinto et al. 2019) showed paternal continuity through time and kinship between individuals buried in the same megalith, as well as between some individuals from different Irish megaliths. Not until full in-depth aDNA studies of a single British long cairn from Hazleton North from around 3700 BC did it become possible to document genetic mating patterns in some detail that could be linked to possible kinship principles among megalithic communities in northwestern Europe (Fowler et al. 2021). Among sixty-six individuals, it was possible to extract sufficient DNA from twenty-six to document a five-generation family burial practice where biological kinship could be demonstrated. It is worth citing the main results:

> Patrilineal descent was key in determining who was buried in the tomb, as all inter-generational transmissions were through men. The presence of women who had reproduced with lineage men and the absence of adult lineage daughters suggests virilocal burial and female exogamy. Combining archaeo-logical and genetic analyses, we demonstrate that one male progenitor repro-duced with four women: the descendants of two of those women were buried in the same half of the tomb over all generations. This suggests that maternal sub-lineages were grouped into branches whose distinctiveness was recog-nized during the tomb's construction. Four males descended from non-lineage fathers and mothers who also reproduced with lineage males, suggesting that some men adopted their reproductive partners' children by other males into their patriline. Ten individuals were not close biological relatives of the main lineage, suggesting that kinship also encompassed social bonds independent of biological relatedness. (Fowler et al. 2021: 1)

From this study, we learn of a complex kinship structure where several principles are combined. The family group descended from one male and his offspring with four women. Even if patrilineal descent was dominant, women held strong ritual positions, which might suggest this to be true in social life, as they could bring their children with other men into the clan. In fact, the organization of the chamber was based on two female lineage groups (north and south chamber), which must have had both ritual and social significance (leading to speculations of a *longue durée* for this duality in the later twin chambers also in northern Europe). Males, however, could also have offspring with several women, suggesting polygamy or serial marriage/partnerships. It seems clear though that we see a rather inclusive and large clan-like kinship system. While descent was patrilineal, two women represented an important organizing principle of the clan structure. In the cairn were also individuals buried from outside this family group, suggesting that perhaps megaliths could serve as burial ground for a wider segment of society beyond the family. However, they might potentially also be related to those skeletons without DNA analysis. Such questions can only be answered with more studies.

However, a major study of burials from Irish megaliths revealed an interest-ing development over time (Cassidy et al. 2020). More than forty samples were analyzed, and they showed that the introduction of farming and megaliths took place at the same time. The newcomers had their ancestry in Iberia, and advanced maritime colonization must be presumed (Paulsson 2019), since they arrived in large enough numbers to prevent inbreeding, allowing for a rapid colonization. However, after a few hundred years, all efforts were concentrated in the building of a few mega-megaliths, most pronounced in New Grange. I cite from the paper:

> We sampled 44 whole genomes, among which we identify the adult son of a first-degree incestuous union from remains that were discovered within the most elaborate recess of the Newgrange passage tomb. Socially sanctioned matings of this nature are very rare, and are documented almost exclusively among politico- religious elites specifically within polygynous and patrilineal royal families that are headed by God-kings. We identify relatives of this individual within two other major complexes of passage tombs 150 km to the west of Newgrange, as well as dietary differences and fine-scale haplotypic structure (which is unprecedented in resolution for a prehistoric population) between passage tomb samples and the larger dataset, which together imply hierarchy. This elite emerged against a backdrop of rapid maritime colonization that displaced a unique Mesolithic isolate population. (Cassidy et al. 2020)

Thus, the elites of these few megalithic centers were related and had formed a super chiefly stratum of their own. It represents the ultimate hierarchization of Neolithic megalithic society, reminiscent of "royal" elites in Hawaii and similar kingdoms around the world (Graeber and Sahlins 2018). Interestingly, it stands in stark contrast to the more collective organization of megasettlements of the Tripolje culture in Ukraine (Müller et al. 2018). They represent two different Neolithic trajectories, neither of which survived after 3000 BC.

This Neolithic kinship pattern also contrasts markedly with third-millennium kinship systems of the Corded Ware and Bell Beakers groups that were introduced through land-based migrations originally from the steppes. Originating from a pastoral, or rather nomadic, economy (Anthony 2022; Knipper et al. 2020; Wilkin et al. 2021), one should of course expect some fundamental differences related to a more movable and dispersed social life linked to animals rather than land, but also social and cultural admixture once they moved into Neolithic Europe. First and most fundamentally, the burial ritual expressed a concern with the individual rather than the collective, and we must assume this also reflected social realities of individual ownership of animals. Male burials were also clearly in the majority. From analyzed Corded Ware cemeteries in south Germany, it became clear that, after settling down, males were mostly local and women mostly nonlocal, suggesting a patrilineal kinship system with female exogamy (Sjögren et al. 2016).

It could further be demonstrated that several of these women had a Neolithic diet during childhood, thus representing social and genetic admixture with remaining Neolithic communities, later genetically confirmed in southeast Poland (Linderholm et al. 2020). In addition, early Corded Ware burials were also totally male-dominated, which suggested migratory movements of mainly young males. It was presented in the following model (Figure 14), which was later confirmed by genetic evidence (Sorrano 2021). Such a model works well in a situation of continued expansion, partly into new territories, partly into already inhabited Neolithic territories (Figure 15a and 15b). This would variously lead to both peaceful and violent confrontations. Here, Corded Ware groups were able to dominate, but once expansion is ended or blocked, the very same push and pull factors are

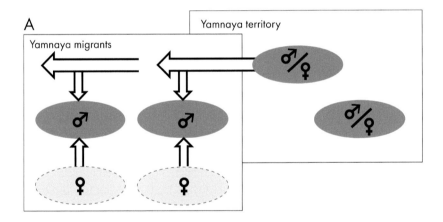

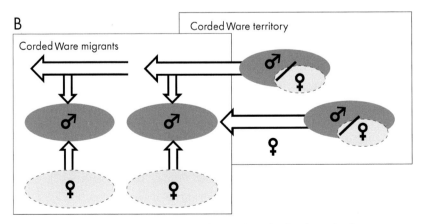

Figure 14 Model of third-millennium BC male-dominated migratory movements (from Kristiansen et al. 2017)

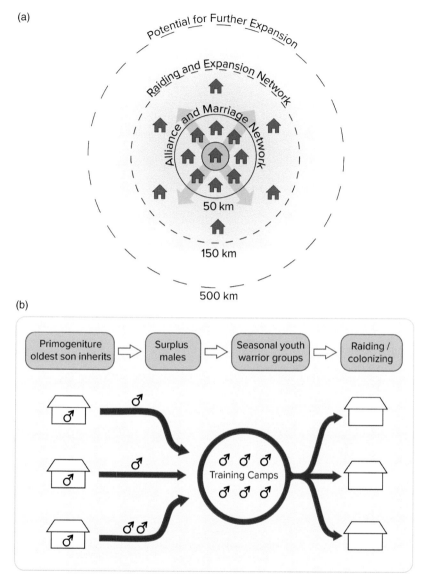

Figure 15a and 15b (a) Geographical model of social worlds of a household during Corded Ware expansion, and (b) a social model of male migratory forces

increasingly replaced by more peaceful alliances based on principles of kinship.

The Corded Ware model of patrilineal, patrilocal residence and female exogamy was later confirmed in a detailed interdisciplinary study of two Bell Beaker cemeteries (Figure 16a and 16b). They showed genetic continuity

(a)

New Settlements

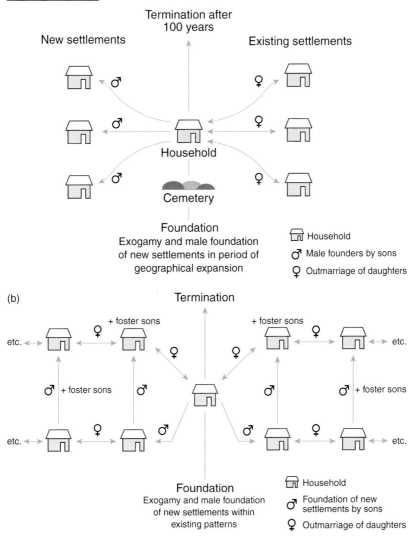

Figure 16a and 16b Model of Bell Beaker settlement and kinship (a) during initial phase, and (b) after settlement consolidation. (From Sjögren et al. 2021)

during four to five generations. One was founded by three brothers, of which only two were married and had offspring. The kinship system was patrilineal and patrilocal, as most males were local, with female exogamy. However, the in-married women all had different haplotypes and thus came from different groups. You did not marry twice with the same group. These principles correspond well with the so-called Omaha kinship system. One example of a returning foster son could be demonstrated, and the evidence suggested monogamous partnerships. Based on this, we propose that the cemeteries represent single households, and we further propose that unfree labor was likely to have been have been part of such households. The model in Figure 16a and 16b demonstrates the dynamics of this kinship system, from the initial expansion stage toward a more consolidated settlement system based on exogamous marriage as well as fosterage.

Bronze Age Kinship Institutions

We can observe some major changes in mobility patterns from the third to the second millennium BC. They correspond to changed patterns of kinship rules, linked to a more ranked society. This growing inequality has been documented genetically and in terms of mobility in a recent study of an Early Bronze Age cemetery from the Lech valley in south Germany (Massy et al. 2017; Mittnik et al. 2019). Here the kinship system was likewise based on patrilineal kinship and female exogamy, but a new form of complexity had emerged. Three groups could be identified in the cemetery. (1) A high-status group of rich male and female burials whose offspring were also richly equipped, indicating that wealth was inherited. Among the group of high-status women, some had married in, but (2) a group of poorly equipped nonlocal women were seen as providing labor in the household, together with some (3) poorly equipped male burials, as it seemed likely that all belonged to the same household (Mittnik et al. 2019). Fosterage was likewise documented.

However, when we reach the Middle Bronze Age of the mid-second millennium BC, the situation has changed again (Kristiansen 2022). Long-distance trade, supported by alliances of confederacies stretching over hundreds of kilometers (Figure 17), provided a stable framework for organized movements and alliances. It meant that both males and females were moving, sometimes long-distance, to form dynastic alliances (Frei et al. 2015 and 2017; Kristiansen et al. 2020). Society is now firmly ranked, with a chiefly elite of free landowners making up 20 percent of the population, buried in elaborate barrows. Nonelites (commoners, and perhaps the unfree) were buried outside barrows in poor flat graves (Bergerbrant et al. 2017). Clearly, the kinship system had become more elaborate and open to adapt to this new reality, which included the institution of guest friendship, crucial for alliances (Kaul 2022). Rowlands describe its role: "A guest friendship between noble households was as binding as marriage, and retained its strength as a bond over several generations" (Rowlands 1980). We find

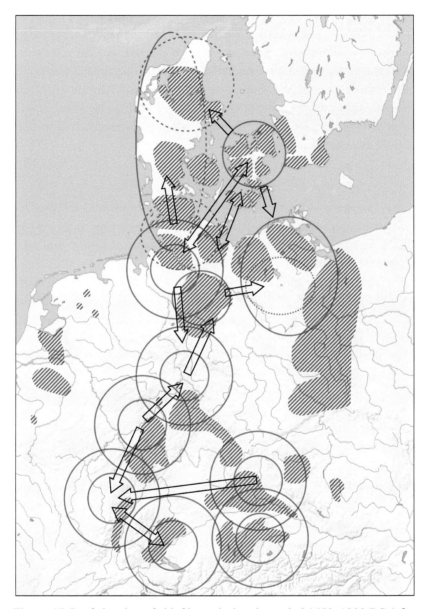

Figure 17 Confederation of chiefdoms during the period 1450–1300 BC (after Kristiansen 2022). Arrows indicate dynastic marriages between neighboring chiefdoms

evidence from written sources in Greece that male elite persons could marry their way into leading positions in foreign dynasties (Finkelberg 2005), and this principle was widely shared throughout Europe (Kristiansen and Larsson 2005: 237). Evidence from later Indo-European sources also makes it likely that the system of fosterage among elite groups was by now highly developed. Different institutions thus supported the movements of warriors, traders, children, and elite women (Figure 18).

In later Celtic and Germanic sources, we find ample evidence of developed systems of fosterage, with roots in the Bronze Age and even earlier. Alliances allow people to travel – that is indeed their rationale, to forge social and economic links between chiefdoms. Such alliances, however, had to be "secured" in more earthly and concrete ways: Marriage would only be a first step. Bride price would be paid for giving away a daughter, but such economic bonds would soon be followed by further social bonds: Foster sons resulting from the alliance would then be placed with the mother's brother's family to further strengthen bonds. Upon his return as an adult, if he returned, the foster son would have forged a foster-brother relationship with one or several of the sons of his mother's brother's family, and such bonds were indeed strong and would last throughout life (Karl 2006 for Celtic sources; for earlier Indo-European sources Olsen 2019). Classic foster brothers were of course Achilles and Patroclus. Fosterage could include both young boys and girls and is well described in Celtic written sources (Karl 2006), but also in older Indo-European linguistic sources (Olsen 2019). Boys would typically be placed with socially superior groups, where they would be brought up and taught the skills of the foster family, whether as a warrior, craftsperson, or learned person (druid, bard). Girls would typically be

Bronze Age Travelers

Who	Warriors	Traders	Kin Groups
Why	raiding and protection	goods and services	marriage and fosterage
How	caravans (land and sea)	caravans (land and sea)	caravans (land and sea)
Social Institution	warrior sodalites / retinues	trade partners guest friendships	marriage alliances/ guest friendships
Political institution	confederations	confederations	confederations
Distances	150–500 km	150–500 km	50–150 km (in confederations ≤ 500 km)

Figure 18 Model of Bronze Age travelers and distances covered (after Kristiansen 2022)

married out to lower-standing groups, already at a young age, so that foster-age and marriage would be part of the same deal. Examples of fosterage is documented in Mittnik et al. (2019, and Bergerbrant 2019), and in the Hungarian Early Bronze Age cemetery at Mokrin (2100–1800 BC) there is evidence already of a more open-ended, less-structured marriage system (Žegarac et al. 2021).

Contrasting Patterns of Kinship

Principles of kinship organize social and economic reproduction in prestate societies. The contrast we have observed so far, admittedly based on rather few case studies, suggests that Neolithic kinship systems from the sixth to the fourth millennium differed markedly from the Copper Age and Bronze Age kinship systems of the third and second millennium BC. It suggests that Neolithic economic strategies adopted a social organization of extended families of cross-cousin marriage, even if the genetic inheritance was patrilineal, but with maternal subgroups, probably linked to a practice of polygamy. Such a system represents an adaptation to economic risks, at least in the initial phases of Neolithic colonization. It also allows women greater power in the household, because a man's heirs are often his sister's children. Patrilineal kinship in combination with smaller core family groups on the other hand grants male heads stronger control over their offspring and heirs, as we see displayed from the third millennium onward, which represents an adaptation to a more decentralized, pastoral economy based on smaller household groups. We should certainly expect to find variation between these two poles (Žegarac et al. 2021), and through time we observe a development during the Bronze Age that opens up both female and male exogamy, meaning that males could marry their way into new households to gain leadership positions, reminding us of the notion of "stranger kings" (Graeber and Sahlins 2018). It represented a response to a much more mobile and open-ended political economy centered on trade. We also observe a trend toward increasing ranking and hierarchy during the Neolithic megalithic culture, possibly linked to increasing endogamy, and some inbreeding, whereas during the Bronze Age a mix of principles allowed more open-ended marriage strategies.

3 Transformation and Migration in Later European Prehistory

Mobility and Migration

In the previous section, I discussed how social mechanisms of kinship and marriage regulated local and regional mobility on a family scale. Now I shall discuss how migration of larger groups can be characterized and documented.

Recent genetic and strontium evidence allows us to characterize different forms of expansion more precisely, not least their genetic and demographic impact, as well as their social organization and interaction with local groups and communities over time (Amorin et al. 2018; Knipper et al. 2017; Mittnik et al. 2019; Sjögren et al. 2021; Veeramah 2018). However, to distill various types of expansion and colonization demands a comparative analysis of archaeological and anthropological cases. Here, I base myself primarily on the work of Anthony (1997), Gosden (2004), Kristinsson (2012), and Bürmeister (2000 and 2019) and on my own work, especially in *Europe before History* (Kristiansen 1998, also Kristiansen 1989). In the following, I delineate different forms of mobility and their genetic and archaeological relationships. Such relationships can take many forms and therefore need to be inferred case by case and then theorized. Likewise, migration is an overarching concept for a variety of expansion types (Kristinsson 2010 and 2012).

Colonizing Expansions/Community Colonization

> The simplest kind of expansion cycle is colonizing expansion. This is triggered when new land becomes available by some historical chance or process such as finding new land that was previously unknown, had become empty for some reason (e.g. previous out-migration) or if new methods were developed that made previously unproductive land suitable for farming. The prime mover here is newly available land. (Kristinsson 2012: 378)

One might also add land occupied by small groups of people, such as hunter-gatherers, who cannot withstand the colonists in numbers, which would have been the case with the Neolithic expansion into Europe. With whole family groups/communities moving en bloc, this is the Neolithic farming colonization of Europe. Recent genetic evidence demonstrates that the LBK groups were full family groups/communities, who were able to mobilize enough labor to clear forests and create new settlements (Shennan 2018). They were genetically the offspring of the original Anatolian farming colonization of Greece and the Balkans (Mathieson et al. 2018); when they reached Hungary, they could no longer sustain large tell communities but split up into smaller communities that became the LBK (Bánffy 2004 and 2019). During the initial colonizing phase, they did not mix with existing hunter-gatherer groups (Szécsényi-Nagy et al. 2014), and afterward only with male hunter-gatherers, it seems (Nikitin et al. 2019). Such behavior corresponds to well-studied ethnographic cases for farmer–hunter-gatherer interaction (Nicolaisen 1976). As has been demonstrated, these colonizing farmers exhibited a remarkable demographic expansion until they reached the economic limits of the system, when warfare and massacres took over. This led to increasing genetic admixture with hunter-gatherers and a new colonizing expansion towards western and northern Europe (Cylenski et al. 2017; Fernandes et al. 2018; Lipson et al. 2017).

Conquest Colonization/System Expansion

The second type of expansion is quite unlike the community-based farming colonization. This type of expansion does not necessarily depend on access to new land but rather represents social systems in constant competition, promoting centrifugal movements of populations into new lands. It is well described among the segmentary Tiv in Africa (Sahlings 1961) but covers most pastoral societies. According to Kristinsson, "system expansions have their origins in competitive systems. These are cultures that show significant levels of conformity and usually, though not always, share a single language. However, they are politically divided which leads to constant and escalating competition between the polities" (2012: 380). Here, we also find the Urnfield expansion of the Late Bronze Age, and most Iron Age migratory expansion, such as the Celtic migrations and later Germanic and Viking migrations. These were the results of an internal development toward increasing militarization, which had to find an outlet:

> Even if these societies were originally based on social stratification and had elite armies they will sooner or later be forced to mobilize the common people in their conflicts. With such militarization comes democratization since the elite cannot effectively subdue or control a populace that is armed and seasoned in war … The common people in such societies are normally a farming population and their greatest political demand is usually the demand for land. (Kristinsson 2012: 380)

This is what Engels called the Germanic mode of production, but it rather represents a stage in a cyclical historical process from the Bronze Age into the Iron Age.

We should divide this type of expansion into two forms: pastoral conquest expansion and farming conquest expansions. They are both in search of new land for grazing and farming or a mix of these, and thus they differ in their economies and in their level of social organization. Pastoral conquest migrations are based on controlling clients, whether other pastoral groups, traders, or farmers, whereas the farming conquest expansions are more typically linked to need for new land and control over subdued clients, who are often made into slaves. In both these cases, we witness a strong male-dominated militarization of society.

Pastoral expansions/conquests are well described in historical and ethnographic literature (Kradin et al. 2003). The later history of the Eurasian steppe typifies such pastoral or nomadic conquest colonization, which over time would lead to gradual linguistic and genetic admixtures or even replacements by new dominant groups (Damgård et al. 2018). However, they are preceded by a more simple yet also male-dominated warrior-based type of migration during the third millennium BC in western Eurasia, typified by the Yamnaya, Corded Ware, and Bell Beaker migrations (Allentoft et al. 2015; Haak et al. 2015; Kristiansen et al. 2017; Olalde et al. 2018).

To minimize risks in a pastoral economy and in exchange for certain products, cattle would have been lent out to networks of partners. We hypothesize that women were exchanged in the opposite direction from animals, and foster sons could be placed with their uncle, a common Indo-European practice that has now also been demonstrated archaeologically in third-millennium Europe (Sjögren et al. 2021; Knipper et al. 2017). Strontium isotopic analyses of several large Corded Ware cemeteries confirm that males remained local, while women were mostly of nonlocal origin and often had a Neolithic diet during childhood (Sjögren et al. 2016; Linderholm et al. 2020).

To conclude, the Yamnaya and Corded Ware cultures had a dominant pastoral mode of production resulting in rapidly expanding, mobile, and low-density populations dependent on animals. This economy continued to dominate into the Bronze Age and led to a long-term increase in a protein-rich diet (Münster et al. 2018: figure 7), with a rapid population increase across Europe, especially after 2000 BC (Müller 2015).

Forces of Change

Economic Drivers and Constraints

Here, I summarize some basic observations about constraints and drivers, which are dialectically related (Figure 19). Thus, constraints may become drivers if societies transform themselves to adapt to new circumstances. We observe this dynamic unfolding when a social and economic system reaches its limits of expansion and then either has to stop or transform to continue expansion into a new social and economic environment. This is also when material culture changes, as social institutions and their cultural markers/identities change. It is exemplified by the transformation of the tell cultures of the Balkan Neolithic (Starčevo-Vinča) into the farmhouse culture of the LBK of central Europe. Eszter Bánffy has located and explained the transformative process in Hungary, when a tell culture of "clayscapes" (all houses were built with clay, useful in a hot and dry environment) was transformed into a house culture of "timberscapes" (timber-built houses, useful in a temperate environment with much forest and rain). The adaptation to a new forest environment was also followed

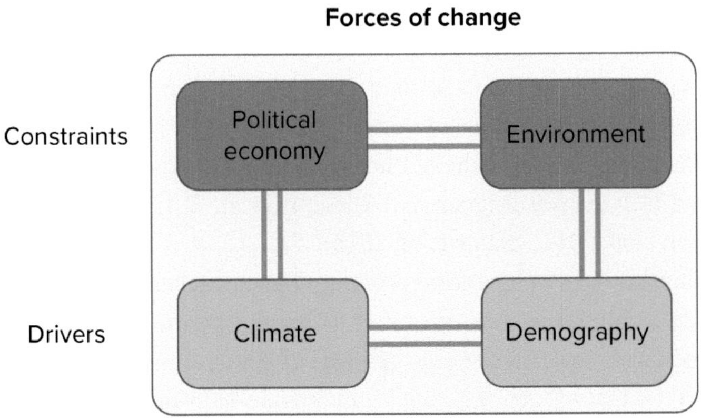

Forces of change

Figure 19 Model showing forces of change and drivers/constraints

by increasing genetic admixture with hunters over time, even if the initial expansion was marked by less admixture (Bánffy 2004 and 2019).

A similar transformation took place when the Yamnaya pastoralists reached the western limit of the steppe in Hungary shortly after 3000 BC and had to stop expanding or adapt to a new economy combining mixed farming with pastoralism in order to cope with a more forested environment. To facilitate this transformation, they would choose flat landscapes with open forest, such as the sandy soils of northwestern Europe; these could more easily be transformed into open steppe-like grazing lands, which happened on a broad scale after 2900 to 2850 BC. However, to expand territories, they displaced or interacted with Neolithic farmers across broad regions of Europe. In central and northern Europe, they interacted through exogamy and female abduction with Neolithic societies (Muhl et al. 2010), and Neolithic women brought with them a new material culture, language, and economy that helped reformulate economic strategies and material culture, becoming the Corded Ware Culture (Juras et al. 2018; Kristiansen et al. 2017). In central Europe, the process was more complex and drawn out (Furtwängler 2020: figure 3).

Finally, conquest migrations of the second and first millennia BC and during the first millennium AD were all based on a militarized society, where warriors were recruited into chiefly retinues that under certain conditions could be mobilized temporarily into larger armies in connection with conquest migrations. Here, constraints and drivers are internal contradictions between increasing hierarchies and a rising male population without access to land and farms. The same forces that fostered expansion in the pastoral mode of production, where sons who could not inherit were sent off as migrating warring colonists, would now lead to more organized raiding and trading expansions, and later conquest and colonization. This could unfold either through maritime forces of raiding and trading, as during the Viking period and the Nordic Bronze Age (Ling et al. 2018), later leading to more massive conquest colonizations, or through land-based conquest migrations, such as those of Central Asia by Andronovo warrior groups after 2000 BC, linked to chariots and well-trained horses (Librado et al. 2021: extended data, figure 6).[4]

Common to the various forms of expansion after 3000 BC is the fact that they share the same social structure based on exogamy in combination with patrilocal and patrilineal kinship systems. With male primogeniture, it fostered strong male-driven expansionist forces, supported from the beginning by shared Indo-European languages, since local continuity, whether matrilocal or patrilocal, determines which language will dominate, as demonstrated in comparative studies (Lansing et al. 2017). We may thus observe a *longue durée* in the basic forces of expansion originating in an Indo-European pastoral social organization of society that prevailed through time, even if the nature and organization of expansion changed. However, we need also to be in command of environmental and climatic knowledge, as well as demographic change. Next, I discuss how recent scientific progress has allowed new insights into the forces of climatic and environmental variations, as well as patterns of demographic change.

Climatic and Demographic Drivers and Constraints

Climate and demography may likewise become drivers once ecological or demographic thresholds are reached. In such a situation, communities can choose to adapt to less favorable conditions or choose ways to provide an outlet for the demographic surplus. Such choices are always dependent on political and social organization, and social revolt may also result as part of the process.

In recent decades, we also have witnessed a small revolution in the fields of climate and environmental research. Pollen diagrams have since the 1950s been constructed by using correction factors for tree pollen, as trees produce a lot

---

[4] It can sometimes be useful to make comparisons with genetic and cultural admixture processes from later periods, where we have written sources to complement the picture. Thus, it seems that the conquest migration of Magyars into Hungary was carried out by relatively small elite groups of East Asian origin, but admixed along the way west; these groups introduced a new language but did not make a strong genetic impact (Neparaczki 2018 and 2019). Like the Avars before them, also of East Asian origin, they retained an elite stratum of mostly endogamous marriage. The Xiongu of East Asia, some of whom later migrated west under the ethnic banner of the Huns, were a genetically admixed group from previously separate late Bronze Age groups, who through political unification by the dominantly East Asian Xiongu entered a period of genetic admixture (Jeong et al. 2020). In some opposition to this historical scenario, the Langobards retained much of their original north European genetic profile during their migrations, and also part of their material culture, linked to elite Langobards (Amorin et al. 2018).

more pollen than other plant species. However, practical experiments with modern pollen production and spread demonstrated that these correction factors had been too conservative, and, in the last twenty years, developments in "real" correction factors have allowed the formulation of a REVEALS model for absolute correction of pollen production in regional pollen diagrams (Sugita 2007). In many ways, this correction program can be paralleled to the C-14 calibration, which meant a real breakthrough for C-14 dating as a precision tool. Calibrating older pollen diagrams "reveals" that changes are not subtle: Landscapes were on the whole a lot more open in later prehistory than previously envisaged. In Figure 20, I show a traditional "relative" pollen diagram from Lake Ove in northwestern Jutland compared to the REVEALS-calibrated version to illustrate this. Pollen diagrams are now increasingly being entered

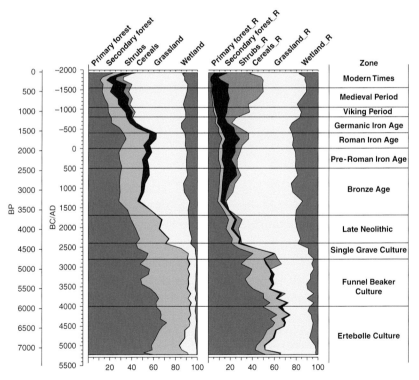

Figure 20 Two versions of the same pollen diagram from Thy in northwestern Jutland. To the left the traditional calibration of forest trees, and to the right the "absolute" REVEALS calibration, which shows the true extent of open land. Here, the decline of the forest with the arrival of the Corded Ware/Single Grave culture groups around 2700 BC becomes much more dramatic (after Kristiansen et al. 2020: figure 20.2)

into a Europe-wide database and can be used in more advanced ways (Fyfe et al. 2009 and 2015). They permit the reconstruction of European-based vegetational histories of openness, but they also allow the illustration of the distribution and frequency of different plant and tree species in time and space. Such data can then be correlated with other types of archaeological or genetic data, as exemplified in Racimo et al. (2020b).

Figure 20 illustrates the effects of the REVEALS calibration by showing a diagram from Thy in northwestern Jutland. Suddenly it becomes clear that the original migration around 2800/2700 BC into Jutland had a much larger effect on the landscape than previously thought: The immigrants simply burned down the forest in a brief time period to create an open grazing landscape for their pastoral economy. It further implies that a large number of both humans and animals must have arrived within a short period of time. In Figure 21, I show the core area of the expansion, and later expansions into eastern Denmark, where migrants now apply megaliths for burials, in a process of increasing cultural admixture.

Finally, we should acknowledge the role of diseases, or rather the disease environment in prehistory, the study of which has also witnessed a revolution, not least in the documentation of the role of plague linked to the spread of the Yamnaya and Corded Ware cultures (Rasmussen et al. 2015). This may have impacted the so-called "Neolithic Decline" and thus paved the way for the steppe migrations (Rascovan et al. 2019). However, epidemics needs to be understood in relation to the social and economic organization of society, which at least in part defines their impact.

4 Towards Interpretative Integration: Cultural, Genetic, and Social Admixture Processes

It has been possible to demonstrate that migrations are of several types, from community colonization to conquest migrations, but we should envisage intermediate forms of both mobility and admixture processes. Each case needs to be studied separately before they can be summed up, in order to extract comparative regularities. Here, I shall make some tentative propositions. It is of utmost importance to keep apart cultural and genetic admixture processes, in order to separate possible causes and effects in the process. For such purposes, it can be useful to make a systematic comparison in the form of charts or tables.

Culture and Genetics

In Figures 22 and 23, I exemplify such an approach. It is a method to simplify the process of change into a few dimensions of admixture in genetics and

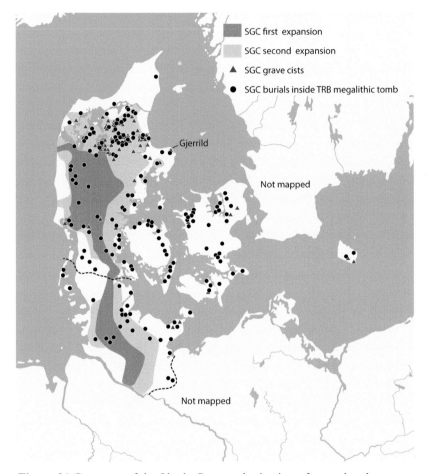

Figure 21 Core area of the Single Grave colonization of central and western
Jutland and its later eastward expansion to the Danish isles, where existing
megaliths were used for burials in a process of cultural and genetic admixture
(after Müller and Vandkilde 2020: figure 2.5)

culture, which can subsequently be quantified when possible. Thus, a general
model is always the starting point from which to document variation from the
model. Here, I start with a chart for genetic and cultural admixture processes at
the transformation from tell culture to LBK (Figure 22). It exemplifies how few
or no changes in genetic admixture processes went along with major changes in
material culture and the organization of households, from the suprahouseholds
of tell society to the scaled-down yet extended households of timber-built
longhouses in the LBK. Continued colonization into a new habitat demanded
a social and economic change, without major genetic change, except some

Tell Culture to LBK

	Genetics	Culture
Type of Admixture	Small male admixture with h/g	new portable culture (pottery, flint technology)
Type of Replacement	mutual avoidance, selective contact with h/g	From clay to timber houses From intra to extra mural burials

Figure 22 Genetic/cultural interaction processes in the LBK

Neolithic to Corded Ware

	Genetics	Culture
Type of Admixture	Admixture in female lines with farmers	Admixture in portable culture and agriculture
Type of Replacement	Neolithic male lines replaced	Burial rituals replaced or modified

Figure 23 Genetic/cultural interaction processes in the Corded Ware culture

small-scale admixture with male hunter-gatherers probably serving as scouts in the process of penetrating into the new forested habitat.

For the change from Neolithic to Corded Ware in temperate central/ northern Europe, we have previously outlined a model that takes into account changes in portable material culture along with continuation of burial ritual, with genetic admixture along Neolithic female lines but no admixture along male lines (Kristiansen et al. 2017). In response to our model of Corded Ware social organization, Martin Furholt has repeatedly suggested that such general models do not catch all local and regional variations in Corded Ware material culture (Furholt 2019). The point I wish to make here is that generalized systems of kinship and social organization coexist along with more local variation in material culture. Furholt's own model of shared burial rituals (figure 10), represents a shared ritual institution that coexisted with other types of regional cultural/ genetic variation, depending on variations in interaction with local Neolithic societies (Furtwängler 2020; Linderholm et al. 2020), yet to be explored in greater detail (Haak et al. in press).

Taken together, I propose that shorter periods of high mobility, conquest, unrest, and social change were followed by longer periods of relative piece, organized mobility, and social consolidation. It raises the important "why" question: Why is it that human communities cannot stay content with peaceful conditions once they have lasted for a sustained period? Here, a number of classic causes enter the scene: the role of climatic change, economic practices that are unsustainable in the long term, demographic forces, and rising social inequalities. Prehistory offers a rich laboratory for testing under which conditions one or the other cause will likely prevail, and such lessons of the past may also be useful for understanding the present. However, the swing of the historical pendulum between war and peace reveals the dialectic forces of history. As I stated in *Europe before History*, "drama and disruption were always essential ingredients in history, lifting it up into memory. Although history was shaped by the accumulating forces of everyday life, its traces and memories were often produced by the unusual and the dramatic. The archaeologist has to situate her- or himself between these two poles" (Kristiansen 1998: 358). To do that effectively, we need to situate war and peace in their proper institutional framework.

The Dialectics of War and Peace

Here, I wish to propose that peace and war represent opposing yet dependent and institutionalized forces (Figures 24 and 25). Prehistoric warfare was just as institutionalized and controlled as marriage and kinship (Anderson 2018; Horn and Kristiansen 2018). But they are also formed and reshaped through time by everyday realities, bending and compromising rules yet pretending still to follow them. Warriors had to be controlled so as not to disturb or destroy their own home base, and therefore their activities had to be regulated, to create an outlet that turned warfare and raiding into benefits, such as providing cattle and women from competing communities (Lincoln 1981). However, loyalties may change over time, and new alliances might turn former competitors into allies. Demographic pressure may also invite conquest migration as an outlet. Indo-European sources, which originated in the Bronze Age but certainly must have changed over time before they were finally written down, document all of these mechanisms.

We can also observe that more violent and uncontrolled warfare increased in periods of tension and competition, whether over land or other resources. As in

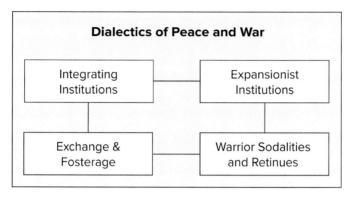

Figure 24 The institutionalized dialectics of war and peace

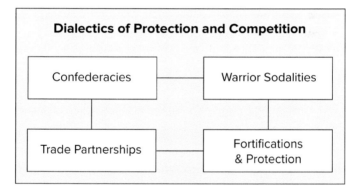

Figure 25 Dialectics of protection and competition

the earlier Neolithic, this can be linked to demographic competition. During the Neolithic, we observe a temporal trend in which deathly violence and massacres prevail during periods of population pressure and competition over resources (Downey et al. 2016), such as the late LBK before its collapse (Meyer et al. 2018a and 2018b), and also during the following expansion period of the Late Neolithic societies, when competition for land increased (Chenal et al. 2015). Thus, during the late LBK, enclosures become more numerous and grow in size during the crisis period (Shennan 2018: figure 4.9). Massacres are of two kinds: execution of whole local communities to take over their territory or selective execution of males, where it is assumed that women are taken as captives, a normal practice well documented ethnographically and historically in prestate societies (Cameron 2016). The same pattern continues during the later Neolithic period (Chenal et al. 2015) and prevailed during periods of internal stress and/or expansion of new groups into already occupied territories (Schroeder et al. 2019).

Another pattern prevailed during the steppe migrations of the earlier third millennium BC. Thus, we can document a male-dominated migratory expansion from Yamnaya to Corded Ware culture, based on two institutionalized principles: that of primogeniture (oldest son inherits) and that of male youth warbands, both well documented in written sources as well as in archaeology (Brown and Anthony 2019). These two institutions created a strong motivation for young males to migrate in order to set up their own households and families, rather than becoming dependent labor under their brother's household. One may even propose that it was the maintenance of these two institutions that gave rise to continued migrations during subsequent millennia. However, from the second millennium BC onward, the youth warbands became institutionalized under chiefly retinues, while still allowing young males to move away and be hired outside the chief's own household. Now it became an organized career strategy, where powerful chiefs would recruit warriors from many different places, as indicated by their varied strontium signatures (Wahl and Price 2013; Price et al 2017).

5 Concluding Perspective

In conclusion, I shall reflect upon new ways of retheorizing commonly used concepts that should follow from the recasting of European prehistory and, on a wider scale, world prehistory. Partly as a reaction to World System theory, the postcolonial movement emerged in response to grand narratives in Western history-writing in the humanities and social sciences. A key point was the reinstitution of local agency during processes of colonization, and following from that, a more balanced understanding of the dialectic forces between colonizers and colonized in their local contexts, not least in the ancient Mediterranean (Hodos 2006; Dietler 2010; Van Dommelen and Knapp 2010). Researchers in anthropology and archaeology began applying ideas from such approaches to prehistoric trade and interaction (Agbe-Davies and Bauer 2010), which also included the popular concept of "hybridity" resulting from resisting violence and oppression (Van Dommelen 2005). However, a growing critique of the postcolonial discourse pointed to its inability to account for exploitation (Monroe 2018) and that the vagueness of some core concepts from this discourse, such as hybridity, ambiguity, and liminality, tends to conceal patterns of dominance and social inequality (Silliman 2015). Therefore, Stockhammer proposed to replace "hybridity" with "entanglement" (Stockhammer 2012). Others, however, have pointed to ways of reconciling Marxist and postcolonial approaches (Sinha and Varma 2015). The point I wish to make is that the third science revolution has opened doors to essential new evidence, which may inspire a rethinking of such theoretical concepts. Following from this, the concept of colonization can and should be employed more widely in prehistory (Gosden 2004). Neolithic farmers were colonizing new land at the expense of existing hunter-gatherers with whom they had no or little interaction, genetically and culturally, until much later. It exhibits all the traditional signs of a civilizational enterprise defining us against them. Superior versus inferior. While it clearly represented a mode of production that unified all Neolithic groups, it also embodied a civilizational enterprise based on a set of culturally defined values from diet to a specific lifestyle, which we may term a Neolithic civilization (Rowlands and Fuller 2018). Thus, mode of production and civilization represent two sides of the same coin, and by applying such a wider definition of both concepts, we escape the inherent notions of progress linked to the idea of civilization as representing only the time from Bronze Age state formation onward. Clearly, this represents another watershed in terms of technological and institutional complexity, but one may suggest that other complexities define other types of unifying cultural and economic formations throughout prehistory and later history (Feuchtwang and Rowlands 2019).

I predict that we are entering a new phase of inspired and theoretically informed interpretations, where a new transdisciplinary discourse of archaeogenetic evidence will allow a reinvigoration of a number of theoretical approaches beyond those discussed in this book. However, such endeavors need to be anchored in a comparative approach (Smith 2012). This is not to say that we should avoid discussing political issues and their possible impact on interpretation; as I have argued, archaeology remains part of the wider discourses in the social sciences and humanities. This is essential for our ability to contribute and critically transmit knowledge from the past to the present. Even if we cannot learn directly from history, we can certainly learn from the forces that shaped it.

References

Agbe-Davies, A. and A. Bauer. 2010. Rethinking Trade as a Social Activity: An Introduction. In A. Bauer and A. S. Agbe-Davies, eds., *Social Archaeologies of Trade and Exchange. Exploring Relationships among People, Places and Things*, 13–28. Walnut Creek, CA: Left Coast Press.

Allentoft, M. E. et al. 2015. Population Genomics of Bronze Age Eurasia. *Nature* 522: 167–72. https://doi.org/10.1038/nature14507.

Allentoft, M. E. et al. 2022. Population Genomics of Stone Age Eurasia. BioRxiv. https://doi.org/10.1101/2022.05.04.490594.

Almagro-Gorbea, M. and A. J. Lorrio Alvarado. 2011. *Teutates. El Heroe Fundador y el culto heroico al antepasado en Hispania y en la Keltiké.* Bibliotheca Archaeologica Hispana 36. Madrid: Real Academia de la Historia.

Alvarez-Sanchís, J. 1999. *Los Vettones*. Madrid: Real Academia de la Historia.

Alvarez-Sanchís, J. 2002. The Iron Age in Western Spain (800 BC–AD 50): An Overview. *Oxford Journal of Archaeology* 19.1: 65–89.

Ammerman, A. J. and L. L. Cavalli-Sforza. 1984. *The Neolithic Transition and the Genetics of Population in Europe*. Princeton, NJ: Princeton University Press.

Amorin, C. E. G. et al. 2018. Understanding 6th-Century Barbarian Social Organization and Migration through Paleogenomics. *Nature Communications* 9: 3547. https://doi.org/10.1038/s41467-018-06024-4.

Anderson, K. 2018. Becoming the Warrior: Constructed Identity or Functional Identity. In C. Horn and K. Kristiansen, eds., *Warfare in Bronze Age Society*, 213–28. Cambridge: Cambridge University Press.

Anthony, D. W. 1997. Prehistoric Migration as Social Process. In J. Chapman and Helena Hamerow, eds., *Migrations and Invasions in Archaeological Explanation*, 21–32. British Archaeological Reports International Series 664. Oxford: BAR.

Anthony, D. 2022. Migration, Ancient DNA, and Bronze Age Pastoralists from the Eurasian Steppes. In M. Daniels, ed., *Homo Migrans: Modeling Mobility and Migration in Human History*. IEMA Distinguished Monograph Series. Albany: SUNY-Press.

Armit, I. and D. Reich. 2020. The Return of the Beaker Folk? Rethinking Migration and Population Change in British Prehistory. *Antiquity*: 1–14. https://doi.org/10.15184/aqy.2021.129.

Arponen, V. P. J. et al. 2019a. Environmental Determinism and Archaeology. Understanding and Evaluating Determinism in Research Design.

Archaeological Dialogues 26: 1–9. https://doi.org/10.1017/S13802038 19000059.

Arponen, V. P. J., et al. 2019b. Two Cultures in the Times of Interdisciplinary Archaeology. A Response to Commentators. *Archaeological Dialogues* 26: 19–24.

Arponen, V. P. J. et al. 2019c. Between Natural and Human Sciences: On the Role and Character of Theory in Socio-Environmental Archaeology. *The Holocene*, special issue: 1–6.

Bánffy, E. 2004. *The 6th Millennium BC Boundary in Western Transdanubia and Its Role in the Central European Transition. The Szentgyörgyvölgyi-Pityerdomb Settlement*. Budapest: Archaeological Institute of the HAS.

Bánffy, E. 2019. *First Farmers of the Carpathian Basin. Changing Patterns in Subsistence, Ritual and Monumental Figurines*. Prehistoric Society Research Paper 8. Oxford: Oxbow Books.

Barrett, J. 2014. The Material Constitution of Humanness. *Archaeological Dialogues* 21: 65–74.

Barrett, J. 2019. The Archaeology of Population Dynamics. *Current Swedish Archaeology* 27: 37–51.

Barth, F. 1969a. Introduction. In F. Barth, ed., *Ethnic Groups and Boundaries: The Social Organization of Culture Difference*, 9–38. London: Allen & Unwin.

Barth, F., ed. 1969b. *Ethnic Groups and Boundaries. The Social Organization of Culture Difference*. London: Allen & Unwin.

Baudou, E. 2005. Kossinna Meets the Nordic Archaeologists. *Current Swedish Archaeology* 13: 121–39.

Baudou, E. 2012. *Oscar Montelius. Om tidens återkomst och kulturens vandringar*. Stockholm: Atlantis.

Bentley, R. A. et al. 2012. Community Differentiation and Kinship among Europe's First Farmers. *PNAS* 109.24: 62–4.

Bergerbrant, S. 2019. Transcultural Fostering in the Bronze Age? A Case Study of Grave 4/2 in Mound II at Abbekås, Sweden. In C. Ljung, A. Andreasson Sjögren, I. Berg, et al., *"Tidens landskap." En vänbok til Anders Andren*, 62–4. Stockholm: Nordic Academic Press.

Bergerbrant, S. et al. 2017. Identifying Commoners in the Early Bronze Age: Burials outside Barrows. In S. Bergerbrant and A. Wessman, eds., *New Perspectives on the Bronze Age. Proceedings of the 13th Nordic Bronze Age Symposium, Held in Gothenburg 9th June to 13th June 2015*, 37–64. Oxford: Archaeopress.

Bickle, P. et al. 2016. At Home in the Neolithic: Understanding Diversity in Neolithic Houses and Households. *Open Archaeology* 2: 410–16.

Bintliff, J. 1999. Structure, Contingency, Narrative and Timelessness. In J. Bintliff, ed., *Structure and Contingency. Evolutionary Processes in Life and Human Society*, 132–48. London: Leicester University Press.

Blake, M. 2020. On the Biodeterministic Imagination. *Archaeological Dialogues* 27: 1–16.

Blanko-Gonzales, A. et al. 2018. Cultural, Demographic and Environmental Dynamics of the Copper and Early Bronze Age in Iberia (3300–1500 BC). Towards an Interregional Multiproxy Comparison at the Time of the 4.2 ky BP Event. *Journal of World Prehistory* 31: 1–79. https://doi.org/10.1007/s10963-018–9113-3.

Boas, F. 1911. *The Mind of Primitive Man*. New York: Macmillan.

Bojs, K. 2017. *My European Family. The First 54,000 Years*. London: Bloomsbury Sigma.

Bondarenko, D. M. et al., eds. 2020. London: Springer.

Booth, T. J. 2019. A Stranger in a Strange Land: A Perspective on Archaeological Responses to the Palaeogenetic Revolution from an Archaeologist Working amongst Palaeogeneticists. *World Archaeology*. https://doi.org/10.1080/00438243.2019.1627240.

Booth, T. J. 2020. Imagined Biodeterminism? *Archaeological Dialogues* 27: 16–19.

Booth, T. J., et al. 2020. Tales from the Supplementary Information: Ancestry Change in Chalcolithic–Early Bronze Age Britain Was Gradual with Varied Kinship Organization. *Cambridge Archaeological Journal*: 1–22.

Bourgeois, Q. and E. J. Kroon. 2017 The Impact of Male Burials on the Construction of Corded Ware Identity: Reconstructing Networks of Information in the 3rd Millennium BC. *PLoS ONE* 12.10: e0185971. https://doi.org/10.1371/journal. pone.018597.

Brown, D. and D. Anthony. 2019. Late Bronze Age Midwinter Dog Sacrifices and Warrior Initiations at Krasnosamarskoe, Russia. In B. A. Olsen et al., eds., *Tracing the Indo-Europeans. New Evidence from Archaeology and Historical Linguistics*, 197–222. Oxford: Oxbow Books.

Bürmeister, S. 2000. Archaeology and Migration. Approaches to an Archaeological Proof of Migration. *Current Anthropology* 41: 539–67. https://doi.org/10.1086/317383.

Bürmeister, S. 2019. Archaeological Migration Research Is Interdisciplinary or It Is Nothing. Ten Essentials How to Think About the Archaeological Study of Migration. In V. I. Molodin and L. N. Mylnikova, eds., *Mobilität und Migration. Konzepte und Methoden, Ergebnisse / Mobility and Migration. Concepts, Methods, Results*. Novosibirsk. DOI: 10.17746/0301-5.2019.229-237

Bürmeister, S. 2021. Does the Concept of Genetic Ancestry Reinforce Racism? *TATuP* 30.2: 41–6. https://doi.org/10.14512/tatup.30.2.41.

Bürmeister, S. and N. Müller-Schessel, eds. 2007. *Soziale Gruppen, Kulturelle Grenzen. Die Interpretation sozialer Identitäten in der prähistorischen Archäologie*. Münster: Waxman Verlag.

Callaway, H. 2018. The Battle for Common Ground. *Nature* 555: 574–6.

Cameron, C. M. 2016. *Captives. How Stolen People Changed the World*. Lincoln: University of Nebraska Press.

Cassidy, L. M. et al. 2020. A Dynastic Elite in Monumental Neolithic Society. *Nature* 582: 384–8.

Chapman, J. 2020. *Forging Identities in the Prehistory of Old Europe. Dividuals, Individuals and Communities 7000–3000 BC*. Leiden:Sidestone Press.

Chenal. F. et al. 2015 A Farewell to Arms: A Deposit of Human Limbs and Bodies at Bergheim, France, c. 4000 BC. *Antiquity* 89: 1313–30.

Chrisomalis, S. and B. Trigger. 2003. Reconstructing Prehistoric Ethnicity: Problems and Possibilities. In J. V. Wright and J.-L. Pilon, eds., *A Passion for the Past. Papers in Honour of James F. Pendergast*. Archaeological Survey of Canada Mercury Series Paper No.164. Gatineau: Canadian Museum of Civilization.

Cifani, G. and S. Stoddart, eds. 2012. *Landscape, Ethnicity and Identity in the Archaic Mediterranean Area*. Oxford: Oxbow Books.

Clarke, D. 1968. *Analytical Archaeology*. London: Methuen.

Clarke, D. 1973. Archaeology: The Loss of Innocence. *Antiquity* 47: 6–18.

Cleere, H., ed. 1984. *Approaches to the Archaeological Heritage*. Cambridge: Cambridge University Press.

Cleere, H. ed. 1989. *Archaeological Heritage Management in the Modern World*. London: Unwin Hyman.

Coole, D. H. and S. Frost. 2010. *New Materialisms. Ontology, Agency, and Politics*. Durham, NC: Duke University Press. https://doi.org/10.1215/9780822392996.

Crellin, R. J. and Harris, O. J. T. 2020. Beyond Binaries. Interrogating Ancient DNA. *Archaeological Dialogues* 27: 37–56.

Curta, F. 2014. Ethnic Identity and Archaeology. In C. Smith, ed., *Encyclopedia of Global Archaeology*. Springer.

Cylenski, M. et al. 2017. Late Danubian Mitochondrial Genomes Shed Light into the Neolithisation of Central Europe in the 5th Millennium BC, *BMC Evolutionary Biology* 17.80. https://doi.org/10.1186/s12862-017-0924-0.

Damgård, P. de Barros et al. 2018. 137 Ancient Human Genomes from across the Eurasian Steppes. *Nature*. https://doi.org/10.1038/s41586-018-0094-2.

Demoule, J.-P. 2012. *Mais où sont passés les Indo-Européens? Le mythe d'origine de l'Occident*. Paris: Seuil.

Díaz de Liaño, G. and M. Fernández-Götz. 2021. Posthumanism, New Humanism and Beyond. *Cambridge Archaeological Journal* 31.3: 543–9.

Díaz-Andreu García, M. 2007. *A World History of Nineteenth-Century Archaeology: Nationalism, Colonialism, and the Past*. Oxford: Oxford University Press.

Díaz-Andreu, M. and T. Champion, eds. 1996. *Nationalism and Archaeology in Europe*. London: UCL Press.

Díaz-Andreu, M. and L. Coltofean-Arizancu. 2021. Interdisciplinarity and Archaeology. A Historical Introduction. In L. Coltofean-Arizancu and M. Díaz-Andreu, eds., *Interdisciplinarity and Archaeology: Scientific Interactions in Nineteenth- and Twentieth-Century Archaeology*, 1–21. Oxford: Oxbow.

Dietler, M. 2010. *Archaeologies of Colonianism. Consumption, Entanglement, and Violence in the Ancient Mediterranean*. Oakland: University of California Press.

Downey, S. S. et al. 2016. European Neolithic Societies Showed Early Warning Signals of Population Collapse. *PNAS* 113.35: 9751–6. www.pnas.org/cgi/doi/10.1073/pnas.1602504113.

Dueck, D. 2012. *Geography in Classical Antiquity*. Cambridge: Cambridge University Press.

Eggers, H. J. 1959. *Einführung in die Vorgeschichte*. Munich: E. Pipers.

Eisenmann, S. et al. 2018. Reconciling Material Cultures in Archaeology with Genetic Data: The Nomenclature of Clusters Emerging from Archaeogenomic Analysis. *Nature Scientific Reports* 8: 13003. https://doi.org/10.1038/s41598-018-31123-z.

Fernandes, D. M. et al. 2018. Agenomic Neolithic Time Transect of Hunter-Farmer Admixture in Central Poland. *Nature Scientific Reports* 8: 14879. https://doi.org/10.1038/s41598-018–33067-w.

Fernández-Götz, M. 2013. Revisiting Iron Age Ethnicity. *European Journal of Archaeology* 16.1: 116–36.

Fernández-Götz, M. and G. Ruiz Zapatero. 2011. Hacia una arqueologia de la etnicidad. *Trabajos de Prehistoria* 68.2: 219–36.

Feuchtwang, S. and M. Rowlands. 2019. *Civilisation Recast. Theoretical and Historical Perspectives*. Cambridge: Cambridge University Press.

Finkelberg, M. 2005. *Greeks and Pre-Greeks: Aegean Prehistory and Greek Heroic Tradition*. Cambridge: Cambridge University Press.

Fischer, A. and K. Kristiansen, eds. 2002. *The Neolithisation of Denmark: 150 Years of Debate*. Sheffield: J. R. Collis.

Fowler, C. et al. 2021. Kinship Practices in a Five-Generation Family from Neolithic Britain: Patrilineal Descent, Maternal Sub-Lineages, Adoptive Sons and Virilocal Burial. *Nature*. https://doi.org/10.1038/s41586-021-04241-4.

Frei, K. M. et al. 2015. Tracing the Life Story of a Bronze Age Girl with High Societal Status. *Nature Scientific Reports* 5: 10431.

Frei, K. M. et al. 2017. A Matter of Months: High Precision Migration Chronology of a Bronze Age Female. *PLoS One* 12.6: e0178834.

Frei, K. M. et al. 2019. Mapping Human Mobility during the Third and Second Millennia BC in Present-Day Denmark. *PLoS ONE* 14.8: e0219850. https://doi.org/10.1371/journal.pone.0219850.

Friedman J., 1975. Tribes, States, and Transformation. In M. Bloch, ed., *Marxist Analysis and Social Anthropology*, 161–202. London: Malaby Press.

Frieman, C. J. and D. Hofmann. 2019. Present Pasts in the Archaeology of Genetics, Identity, and Migration in Europe: A Critical Essay, *World Archaeology*, https://doi.org/10.1080/00438243.2019.1627907.

Furholt, M. 2008. Pottery, Cultures, People? The European Baden Material Re-examined. *Antiquity* 82: 614–28.

Furholt, M. 2017. Translocal Communities. Exploring Mobility and Migration in Sedentary Societies of the European Neolithic and Early Bronze Age. *Praehistorische Zeitschrift* 92.2: 304–21.

Furholt, M. 2018 Massive Migrations? The Impact of Recent aDNA Studies on our View of Third Millennium Europe. *European Journal of Archaeology* 21.2: 159–91.

Furholt, M. 2019 Re-integrating Archaeology: A Contribution to aDNA Studies and the Migration Discourse on the 3rd Millennium BC in Europe. *Proceedings of the Prehistoric Society* 85: 115–29. https://doi.org/10.1017/ppr.2019.4.

Furholt, M. 2020. Biodeterminism and Pseudo-objectivity as Obstacles for the Emerging Field of Archaeogenetics. *Archaeological Dialogues* 27: 23–5.

Furholt, M. 2021. Mobility and Social Change: Understanding the European Neolithic Period after the Archaeogenetic Revolution. *Journal of Archaeological Research*. https://doi.org/10.1007/s10814-020-09153-x.

Furtwängler, A. et al. 2020. Ancient Genomes Reveal Social and Genetic Structure of Late Neolithic Switzerland. *Nature Communications* 11. https://doi.org/10.1038/s41467-020–15560-x.

Fyfe, R. M. et al. 2009. The European Pollen Database: Past Efforts and Current Activities. *Vegetation History and Archaeobotany* 18: 417.

Fyfe, R. et al. 2015. From Forest to Farmland: Pollen-Inferred Land Cover Change across Europe Using the Pseudobiomization Approach. *Global Change Biology* 21: 1197–212. https://doi.org/10.1111/gcb.12776.

Gailey, C. W. 1987. *Kinship to Kingship. Gender Hierarchy and State Formation in the Tongan Islands*. Austin: University of Texas Press.

Gardner, A. et al., eds. 2013– . *The Oxford Handbook of Archaeological Theory*. Oxford: Oxford University Press.

Gell, A. 1998. *Art and Agency. An Anthropological Theory*. Oxford: Clarendon Press.

Gibson, B. D. 2011. Chiefdom Confederacies and State Origins. *Social Evolution & History* 10.1: 215–33.

Goldhahn, J. 2019. *Birds in the Bronze Age*. Cambridge: Cambridge University Press.

Gosden, C. 1999. *Anthropology & Archaeology. A Changing Relationship*. London: Routledge.

Gosden, C. 2004. *Archaeology and Colonialism. Cultural Contact from 5000 BC to the Present*. Cambridge: Cambridge University Press.

Gould, S. J. 1999. Introduction: The Scales of Contingency and Punctuation in History. In J. Bintliff, ed., *Structure and Contingency. Evolutionary Processes in Life and Human Society*, x–xxii. London: Leicester University Press.

Graeber, D. and M. Sahlins. 2018. *On Kings*. Chicago: Hau Books.

Grayson, D. K. 1983. *The Establishment of Human Antiquity*. New York: Academic Press.

Green, R. E. et al. 2010. A Draft Sequence of the Neandertal Genome. *Science* 328.5979, May 7: 710–22. https://doi.org/10.1126/science.1188021.

Haak, W. et al. 2015. Massive Migration from the Steppe was a Source for Indo-European Languages in Europe. *Nature* 522: 207–211. https://doi.org/10.1038/nature14317.

Haak, W. et al. 2022. The Corded Ware Complex in Europe in Light of Current Archaeogenetic and Environmental Evidence. In K. Kristiansen, G. Kroonen, and E. Willerslev, eds., *The Indo-European Puzzle Revisited: Integrating Archaeology, Genetics, and Linguistics*. Cambridge: Cambridge University Press.

Hakenbeck, S. E. 2019. Genetics, Archaeology and the Far Right: An Unholy Trinity. *World Archaeology*. https://doi.org/0.1080/00438243.2019.1617189.

Hall, J. 1997. *Ethnic Identity in Greek Antiquity*. Cambridge: Cambridge University Press.

Hall, J. 2002. *Hellenicity: Between Ethnicity and Culture*. Chicago: Chicago University Press.

Hansen, S. 2019. Noch einmal: Abschied von den Indogermanen. In V. I. Molodin and L. N. Mylnikova, eds., *Mobilität und Migration. Konzepte und Methoden, Ergebnisse / Mobility and Migration. Concepts, Methods, Results*. Novosibirsk. https://doi.org/10.17746/0301-5.2019.229-237.

Hedeager, L. 2010. *Iron Age Myth and Materiality*. London: Routledge.

Helms, M. W. 1998. *Access to Origins. Affines, Ancestors and Aristocrats*. Austin: University of Texas Press.

Heyd, V. 2017. Kossinna's Smile. *Antiquity* 91: 1–12.

Heyd, V. et al. 2018. Archaeological Background to the Beaker Complex. Supplementary Information to Olalde et al. 2018.

Hinz, M. et al. 2012. Demography and the Intensity of Cultural Activities: An Evaluation of Funnel Beaker Societies (4200–2800 cal BC). *Journal of Archaeological Sciences* 39: 3331–40.

Hodder, I., ed. 1978. *The Spatial Organisation of Culture*. Duckworth, London.

Hodder, I. ed. 1982a. *Symbolic and Structural Archaeology*. Cambridge: Cambridge University Press,.

Hodder, I. 1982b. *Symbols in Action*. Cambridge: Cambridge University Press.

Hodder, I. 1982c. Theoretical Archaeology: A Reactionary View. In Hodder 1982a, 1–17.

Hodder, I. 1990. *The Domestication of Europe*. Oxford: Blackwell.

Hodder, I. 1992. *Theory and Practice in Archaeology*. London: Routledge.

Hodder, I. 2016. *Studies in Human-Thing Entanglement*. Open Access Book.

Hodder, I. and C. Orton. 1976. *Spatial Analysis in Archaeology*. Cambridge: Cambridge University Press.

Hodos, T. 2006. *Local Responses to Colonization in the Iron Age Mediterranean*. London: Routledge.

Hofmann, D. 2019. Commentary. Archaeology, Archaeogenetics and Theory. *Current Swedish Archaeology* 27: 133–40.

Holst, M. K. et al. 2013. Bronze Age "Herostrats": Ritual, Political, and Domestic Economies in Early Bronze Age Denmark. *Proceedings of the Prehistoric Society* 79: 265–96.

Horn, C. and K. Kristiansen, eds. 2018. *Warfare in Bronze Age Society*. Cambridge: Cambridge University Press.

Hornborg, A. 2014. Political Economy, Ethnogenesis, and Language Dispersals in the Prehispanic Andes: A World-System Perspective. *American Anthropologist* 116.4: 810–23.

Hornborg, A. 2016. *Global Magic. Technologies of Appropriation from Ancient Times to Wall Street*. New York: Palgrave Macmillan.

Hornborg, A. and J. D. Hill, eds. 2011. *Ethnicity in Ancient Amazonia. Reconstructing Past Identities from Archaeology, Linguistic and Ethnohistory*. Boulder: University Press of Colorado.

Huggett, J. 2020. Is Big Digital Data Different? Towards a New Archaeological Paradigm. *Journal of Field Archaeology* 45: 8–17. https://doi.org/10.1080/00934690.2020.1713281.

Ion, A. 2017. How Interdisciplinary Is Interdisciplinarity? Revisiting the Impact of aDNA Research for the Archaeology of Human Remains. *Current Swedish Archaeology* 25: 177–98.

Ion, A. 2019. Who Are We as Historical Beings? Shaping Identities in the Light of the Archaeogenetics "Revolution." *Current Swedish Archaeology* 27: 11–36.

Ion, A. in press. Boundary Objects, Identities and Archaeology. *Forum kritische Archäologie*.

Iversen, R. and G. Kroonen. 2017. Talking Neolithic: Linguistic and Archaeological Perspectives on How Indo-European Was Implemented in Southern Scandinavia. *American Journal of Archaeology* 121.4: 511–25.

Jacob-Friesen, K. H. 1928. *Grundfragen der Urgeschichtsforschung. Stand und Kritik der Forschung über Rassen, Völker und Kulturen in urgeschichtlicher Zeit*. Hannover: Hannoversches Provinzialmuseum für Kunst und Wissenschaft.

Jeong, C. et al. 2020. A Dynamic 6,000-Year Genetic History of Eurasia's Eastern Steppe. *Cell* 183: 1–15. https://doi.org/10.1016/j.cell.2020.10.015.

Johnson, K. M. and K. S. Paul. 2016. Bioarchaeology and Kinship: Integrating Theory, Social Relatedness, and Biology in Ancient Family Research. *Journal of Archaeological Research* 24: 75–123.

Jones, S. 1997. *The Archaeology of Ethnicity. Constructing Identities in the Past and the Present*. London: Routledge.

Juras, A. et al. 2018. Mitochondrial Genomes Reveal an East to West Cline of Steppe Ancestry in Corded Ware Populations. *Nature* 8:11603.

Kaliff, A. and T. Oestigaard. 2021. *Werewolves, Warriors and Winter Sacrifices. Unmasking Kivik and Indo-European Cosmology in Bronze Age Scandinavia*. Opia 75, Uppsala: Uppsala University.

Källen, A. et al. 2019. Archaeogenetics in Popular Media. Contemporary Implications of Ancient DNA. *Current Swedish Archaeology* 27: 69–91. https://doi.org/10.37718/CSA.2019.04.

Karl, R. 2006. *Altketische Sozialstruturen*. Budapest: Archaeolingua.

Karl, R. no date. *Neighbourhood, Hospitality, Fosterage and Contracts*. Late Hallstatt and Early La Tène Complex Social Interaction North of the Alps. Academia.edu.

Kaul, F. 2022. Middle Bronze Age Long Distance Exchange: Amber, Early Glass, and Guest Friendship, Xenia. In J. Ling, R. J. Chacon, and K. Kristiansen, eds., *Trade before Civilization*. Cambridge: Cambridge University Press.

Knipper, C. et al. 2017. Female Exogamy and Gene Pool Diversification at the Transition from the Final Neolithic to the Early Bronze Age in Central Europe. *PNAS*. https://doi.org/10.1073/pnas.1706355114.

Knipper, C. et al. 2020. Diet and Subsistence in Bronze Age Pastoral Communities from the Southern Russian Steppes and the North Caucasus. *PLoS ONE* 15.10: e0239861. https://doi.org/10.1371/journal.pone.0239861.

Kohl, P. L. and C. Fawcett. 1995. *Nationalism, Politics, and the Practice of Archaeology*. Cambridge: Cambridge University Press.

Kossinna, G. 1896. Die vorgeschichtliche Ausbreitung der Germanen in Deutschland. *Zeitshcrift des Vereins für Volkskunde* 6: 1–14.

Kossinna, G. 1911. *Die Herkunft der Germanen. Zur Methode der Siedlungsar chäologie*. Manus Bibliothek 6. Leipzig: Verlag von Curt Kabitzsch.

Kradin, N. N. et al., eds. 2003. *Nomadic Pathways in Social Evolution*. Moscow: Center for Civilizational and Regional Studies of the Russian Academy of Sciences.

Krause, J., with T. Trappe. 2019. *Die Reise unserer Gene: Eine Geschichte über uns und unsere Vorfahren*. n.p.: Propyläen.

Kristiansen, K. 1989. Prehistoric Migrations. The Case of the Single Grave and Corded Ware Cultures. *Journal of Danish Archaeology* 8: 211–25.

Kristiansen, K. 1993. "The Strength of the Past and Its Great Might." An Essay on the Use of the Past. *Journal of European Archaeology* 1: 3–32.

Kristiansen, K. 1996. Old Boundaries and New Frontiers: Reflections on the Identity of Archaeology. *Current Swedish Archaeology* 4: 103–22.

Kristiansen, K. 1998. *Europe before History*. Cambridge: Cambridge University Press.

Kristiansen, K. 2002. The Birth of Ecological Archaeology in Denmark: History and Research Environments 1850–2000. In Fischer and Kristiansen 2002, 11–31.

Kristiansen, K. 2004. Genes versus Agents. A Discussion of the Widening Theoretical Gap in Archaeology. *Archaeological Dialogues* 11.2: 77–99.

Kristiansen, K. 2008. The Discipline of Archaeology. In B. Cunliffe, C. Gosden, and R. A. Joyce, eds., *The Oxford Handbook of Archaeology*, 1–46. Oxford: Oxford University Press.

Kristiansen, K. 2011. Constructing Social and Cultural Identities in the Bronze Age. In B. W. Roberts and M. Vander Linden, eds., *Investigating Archaeological Cultures: Material Culture, Variability, and Transmission*, 201–10. London: Springer. https://doi.org/10.1007/978-1-4419-6970-5_10.

Kristiansen, K. 2014a. Bronze Age Identities. From Social to Cultural and Ethnic Identity. In J. McInerney, ed., *A Companion to Ethnicity in the Ancient Mediterranean*, 82–96. Oxford: Wiley Blackwell.

Kristiansen, K. 2014b. Towards a New Paradigm? The Third Science Revolution and Its Possible Consequences in Archaeology. *Current Swedish Archaeology* 22: 11–34.

Kristiansen, K. 2016. Interpreting Bronze Age Trade and Migration. In E. Kiriatzi and C. Knappett, eds., *Human Mobility and Technological Transfer in the Prehistoric Mediterranean*, 154–81. Cambridge: Cambridge University Press.

Kristiansen, K. 2017. The Nature of Archaeological Knowledge and Its Ontological Turns. *Norwegian Archaeological Review* 50: 120–3.

Kristiansen, K. 2019. Who Is Deterministic? On the Nature of Interdisciplinary Research in Archaeology. *Archaeological Dialogues*: 1–3. https://doi.org/10.1017/S1380203819000060.

Kristiansen, K. 2022. Towards a New Prehistory: Re-theorising Genes, Culture and Migratory Expansions. In M. Daniels, ed., *Homo Migrans. Modelling Mobility and Migration in Human History*. IEMA Distinguished Monograph Series. Albany: SUNY Press.

Kristiansen, K. in press. Bronze Age Travelers. In M. Fernández-Götz, C. Nimura, P. Stockhammer, and R. Cartwright, eds., *Rethinking Migrations in Late Prehistoric Eurasia*. Proceedings of the British Academy. Oxford: Oxford University Press.

Kristiansen, K. et al. 2017. Re-theorising Mobility and the Formation of Culture and Language among the Corded Ware Culture in Europe. *Antiquity* 91.356: 334–47.

Kristiansen, K. and T. Earle. 2015. Neolithic versus Bronze Age Social Formations: A Political Economy Approach. In K. Kristiansen, L. Šmejda, and J. Turek, eds., *Paradigm Found. Archaeological Theory. Present, Past and Future. Essays in Honour of Evžen Neustupný*, 234–47. Oxford: Oxbow Books.

Kristiansen, K. and T. Earle. 2022. Modelling Modes of Production: European 3rd and 2nd Millennium BC Economies. In M. Poettinger, M. Fragipane, and B. Schefold, eds., *Ancient Economies in Comparative Perspective*. London: Springer.

Kristiansen, K. and T. B. Larsson. 2005. *The Rise of Bronze Age Society. Travels, Transmission and Transformations*. New York: Cambridge University Press.

Kristiansen, K. et al. 2020. Thy at the Crossroads: A Local Bronze Age Community's Role in a Macro-Economic System. In K. I. Austvoll, M. H. Eriksen, P. D. Fredriksen, L. Melheim, L. Skogstrand, and L. Prøsch-Danielsen, eds., *Contrasts of the Nordic Bronze Age. Essays in Honour of Christopher Prescott*, 269–82. The Archaeology of Northern Europe 1. Turnhout: Brepols.

Kristiansen, K. et al., eds. 2022 *The Indo-European Puzzle Revisited: Integrating Archaeology, Genetics, and Linguistics*. Cambridge: Cambridge University Press.

Kristinsson, A. 2010. *Expansions: Competition and Conquest in Europe Since the Bronze Age*. Reykjavík: Reykjavíkur Akademían.

Kristinsson, A. 2012. Indo-European Expansion Cycles. *The Journal of Indo-European Studies* 40.3–4): 365–433.

Kuhn, T. 1962. *The Structure of Scientific Revolutions*. 2nd ed. Chicago: University of Chicago Press

Kveiborg, J. 2018. Traversing the Sky and the Earth. The Nordic Bronze Age Horse in a Long-Term Perspective. *Praehistorische Zeitschrift* 93.2: 225–64.

Kveiborg, J. 2020. Together or Apart? Identifying Ontologies in the Nordic Bronze and Iron Age through the Study of Human–Horse Relationships. In K. I. Austvoll et al., eds., *Contrasts of the Nordic Bronze Age. Essays in Honour of Christopher Prescott*, 115–27. The Archaeology of Northern Europe 1. Turnhout: Brepols.

Lalueza-Fox, C. 2013. Agreements and Misunderstandings among Three Scientific Fields. *Current Anthropology* 54: 214–20.

Lansing J. S. et al. 2017. Kinship Sructures Create Persistent Channels for Language Transmissions. *Proceedings of the Nationall Academy of Sciences USA* 114.49: 12910–15. https://doi.org/10.1073/pnas.1706416114.

Larsen, C. S. 2014. Life Conditions and Health in Early Farmers. A Global Perspective and Consequences of a Fundamental Transition. In A. Whittle and P. Bickle, eds., *Early Farmers. The View from Archaeology and Science*, 215–32. Proceedings of the British Academy 198. Oxford: The British Academy and Oxford University Press.

Levi-Strauss, C. 1969. *The Elementary Structures of Kinship*. Boston: Beacon Press.

Librado, P. et al. 2021. Genomic Origins and Spread of Domestic Horses from the Bronze Age Western Eurasia Steppe. *Nature*. https://doi.org/10.1038/s41586-021-04018-9.

Liedman, S.-E. 2018. *A World to Win: The Life and Works of Karl Marx*. Verso.

Lincoln, B. 1981. *Priests, Warriors and Cattle. A Study in the Ecology of Religion*. Los Angeles: University of California Press.

Linderholm, A. et al. 2020. Corded Ware Cultural Complexity Uncovered Using Genomic and Isotopic Analysis from South-Eastern Poland. *Nature Scientific Report* 10: 6885. https://doi.org/10.1038/s41598-020-63138-w.

Ling, J., R. Chacon, and K. Kristiansen, eds. 2022. *Trade before Civilization*. Cambridge: Cambridge University Press.

Ling, J. et al. 2018. Maritime Mode of Production. Raiding and Trading in Seafaring Chiefdoms. *Current Anthopology* 59: 515–16. https://doi.org/10.1086/699613.

Lipson, M. et al. 2017. Parallel Palaeogenomic Transects Reveal Complex Genetic History of Early European Farmers. *Nature*. https://doi.org/10.1038/nature24476.

Lucas, G. 2015. The Mobility of Theory. *Current Swedish Archaeology* 23: 13–32.

Lucas, G. 2017. The Paradigm Concept in Archaeology. *World Archaeology* 49: 260–70.

Mace, R. et al., eds. 2005. *The Evolution of Cultural Diversity. A Phylogenetic Approach*. Walnut Creek, CA: Left Coast Press.

Madella, M. et al., eds. 2013. *The Archaeology of Household*. Oxford: Oxbow Books.

Malkin, I. 2014. *A Small Greek World. Networks in the Ancient Mediterranean*. Oxford: Oxford University Press.

Marila, M. M. 2019. Slow Science for Fast Archaeology. *Current Swedish Archaeology* 27: 93–114. https://doi.org/10.37718/CSA.2019.05.

Martinon-Torres, M. and D. Killick. 2015. Archaeological Theories and Archaeological Sciences. In Gardner et al. 2013– .

Marx. K. 1953. *Grundrisse der Kritik der politischen Ökonomie: (Rohentwurf) 1857–1858: Anhang 1850–1859*. Berlin: Dietz.

Marx, K. 1974. *Grundrisse. Foundations of the Critique of Political Economy (Rough Draft)*. London: Penguin Books, in association with New Left Review.

Massy, K. et al. 2017. Patterns of Transformation from the Final Neolithic to the Early Bronze Age: A Case Study from the Lech Valley South of Augsburg. In P. Stockhammer and J. Maran, eds., *Appropriating Innovations. Entangled Knowledge In Eurasia 5000–1500 BC*, 241–61. Oxford: Oxbow Books.

Mathieson, I. et al. 2018. The Genomic History of Southeastern Europe. *Nature*. https://doi.org/10.1038/nature25778.

McCoy, M. D. 2017. Geospatial Big Data and Archaeology: Prospects and Problems Too Great to Ignore. *Journal of Archaeological Science*: 74–94. http://dx.doi.org/10.1016/j.jas.2017.06.003.

McInerney, J., ed. 2014. *A Companion to Ethnicity in the Ancient Mediterranean*. Oxford: Wiley Blackwell.

Meyer, C. et al. 2018a. Early Neolithic Executions Indicated by Clustered Cranial Trauma in the Mass Grave of Halberstadt. *Nature Communications* 9: 2472. https://doi.org/10.1038/s41467-018-04773-w.

Meyer, C. et al. 2018b. Patterns of Collective Violence in the Early Neolithic of Central Europé. In A. Dolfini, R. J. Crellin, C. Horn, and M. Uckelmann, eds., *Prehistoric Warfare and Violence. Quantitative and Qualitative Approaches*, 21–38. Cham: Springer.

Mittnik, A. et al. 2019. Kinship-based Social Inequality in Bronze Age Europe. *Science* 366: 731–4. https://doi.org/10.1126/science.aax6219.

Monroe, C. M. 2018. Marginalizing Civilization: The Phoenician Redefinition of Power circa 1300–800 BC. In K. Kristiansen, T. Lindkvist. and J. Myrdal, eds., *Trade and Civilisation. Economic Networks and Cultural Ties, from Prehistory to the Early Modern Era*, 195–241. Cambridge: Cambridge University Press.

Montelius, O. 1884. Om våra förfäders invandring till Norden. *Nordisk Tidskrift* 1884: 21–36. In German by J. Mestorf (1888). Über die Einwanderung unserer Vorfahren in den Norden, 27: 151–60.

Montelius, O. 1885. *Om tidsbestämning inom bronsåldern med särskildt afseende på Skandinavien.* Kungl. Vitterhets Historie och Antikvitets Akademiens Handlingar 30. Stockholm.

Montelius, O. 1903. *Die typologische Methode.* In *Die älteren Kulturperioden im Orient und in Europa.* Stockholm.

Morgan, L. H. 1877. *Ancient Society.* London: Macmillan.

Muhl, A. et al. 2010. *Tatort Eulau. Ein 4500 Jahre altes Verbrechen wird Aufgeklärt.* Stuttgart: Theiss.

Müller, J. 2015. Eight Million Neolithic Europeans: Social Demography and Social Archaeology on the Scope of Change. From the Near East to Scandinavia. In K. Kristiansen et al., eds., *Paradigm Found. Archaeological Theory. Present, Past and Future. Essays in Honour of Evžen Neustupný*, 200–15. Oxford: Oxbow Books.

Müller, J. and A. Diachenko. 2019. Tracing Long-Term Demographic Changes. The Issue of Spatial Scales. *PLoS ONE* 14: e0208739. https://doi.org/10.1371/journal.pone.0208739.

Müller, J. and H. Vandkilde. 2020. The Nordic Bronze Age Rose from Copper Age Diversity. In K. I. Austvoll et al., eds., *Contrasts of the Nordic Bronze Age. Essays in Honour of Christopher Prescott.* The Archaeology of Northern Europe 1. Turnhout: Brepols.

Müller, J. et al., eds. 2016. *Trypillia Mega-Sites and European Prehistory 4100–3400 BCE.* London: Routledge.

Müller, J., et al. 2018. The Social Constitution and Political Organization of Tripolye Mega-Sites: Hierarchy and Balance. In H. Meller et al., eds., *Surplus without the State. Political Forms in Prehistory.* Tagungen des Landesmuseum für Voergeschichte Halle, Band 18. Halle: Landesmuseum für Voergeschichte Halle.

Müller-Karpe, H. 1985. *Frauen des 13. Jahrhunderts v. Chr.* Kulturgeschichte der Antiken Welt Band 26. Mainz: Phillip von Zabern.

Müller-Karpe, H. 2004. Zur religiösen Symbolik von bronzezeitlichen Trachtschmuck aus Mitteleuropa. *Anados. Studies of the Ancient World* 2003, 3: 145–54.

Münster, A. et al. 2018. 4000 Years of Human Dietary Evolution in Central Germany, from the First Farmers to the First Elites. *PLoS ONE* 13: e0194862. https://doi.org/10.1371/journal.pone.0194862.

Narasimhan, V. et al. 2019. The Formation of Human Populations in South and Central Asia. *Science* 365. https://doi.org/10.1126/science.aat7487.

Nebelsick, L. D. 2005. Ikonographie und Geschlecht: Bilinguale figürliche Darstellungen zwischen Nordischem Kreis und Mitteleuropa. In B. Hänsel et al., eds., *Interpretationsraum Bronzezeit. Bernhard Hänsel von seinen Schüler gewidmet*, 575–98. Bonn: R. Habelt.

Neparáczki, E. et al. 2018. Mitogenomic Data Indicate Admixture Components of Central-Inner Asian and Srubnaya Origin in the Conquering Hungarians. *PLoS ONE* 13.10: e0205920. https://doi.org/10.1371/journal.pone.0205920

Neparáczki, E. et al. 2019. Y-chromosome Haplogroups from Hun, Avar and Conquering Hungarian Period Nomadic People of the Carpathian Basin. *Sci Rep* 9: 16569. https://doi.org/10.1038/s41598-019-53105-5.

Nicolaisen, I., 1976. The Penan of the Seventh Division of Sarawak: Past, Present and Future. *Sarawak Museum Journal* 24.45 n.s: 35–61.

Nikitin, A. G. et al. 2019. Interactions between Earliest Linearbandkeramik Farmers and Central European Hunter Gatherers at the Dawn of European Neolithization. *BioRxiv*. http://dx.doi.org/10.1101/741900.

Nilsson Stutz, L. 2018. A Future for Archaeology: In Defense of an Intellectually Engaged, Collaborative and Confident Archaeology. *Norwegian Archaeological Review* 51.1–2: 48–56. https://doi.org/10.1080/00293652.2018.1544168.

Odner, K. 2000. *Tradition and Transmission. Bantu, Indo-European and Circumpolar Great Traditions*. Bergen Studies in Social Anthropology 54. Bergen: Norse Publications.

Oestigaard, T. and J. Goldhahn. 2006. From the Dead to the Living: Death as Transactions and Re-negotiations. *Norwegian Archaeological Review* 39(1): 27–48.

Olalde, I. et al. 2018. The Beaker Phenomenon and the Genomic Transformation of Northwest Europe. *Nature*. https://doi.org/10.1038/nature25738.

Olsen, B. A. 2019. Aspects of Family Structure among the Indo-Europeans. In B. A. Olsen et al., eds., *Tracing the Indo-Europeans. New Evidence from Archaeology and Historical Linguistics*, 145–64. Oxford: Oxbow Books.

Oma, K. and J. Goldhahn. 2020. Introduction: Human–Animal Relationships from a Long-Term Perspective. *Current Swedish Archaeology* 28: 11–22.

Papac, L. et al. 2021. Dynamic Changes in Genomic and Social Structures in Third Millennium BCE Central Europe. *Science Advances* 7. https://doi.org/10.1126/sciadv.abi6941.

Paulsson, B. S. 2019. Radiocarbon Dates and Bayesian Modeling Support Maritime Diffusion Model for Megaliths in Europe. *PNAS*. www.pnas.org/cgi/doi/10.1073/pnas.1813268116.

Perry, S. and J. S. Taylor. 2018. Theorising the Digital: A Call to Action for the Archaeological Community. In M. Matsumoto and E. Uleberg, eds., *Oceans of Data: Proceedings of the 44th Conference on Computer Applications and Quantitative Methods in Archaeology*, 11–22. Oxford: Archaeopress. https://doi.org/10.1080/00934690.2021.1899889.

Price, D. et al. 2001. Prehistoric Human Migration in the Linearbandkeramik of Central Europe. *Antiquity* 75: 593–603.

Price, T. D. et al. 2017. Multi-isotope Proveniencing of Human Remains from a Bronze Age Battlefield in the Tollense Valley in Northeast Germany. *Archaeological and Anthropological Sciences* 11: 33–49. https://doi.org/10.1007/s12520-017-0529-y.

Przybyla, M. S. 2009. *Intercultural Contacts in the Western Carpathian Area at the Turn of the 2nd and 1st Millennia BC*. Warsaw: Narodowe Centrum Cultury.

Racimo, F. et al. 2020a. Beyond Broad Strokes: Sociocultural Insights from the Study of Ancient Genomes. *Nature Reviews Genetics*. https://doi.org/10.17863/CAM.50029.

Racimo, F. et al. 2020b The Spatiotemporal Spread and Impact of Human Migrations during the European Holocene. *PNAS* 117.16: 8989–9000. https://doi.org/10.1073/pnas.1920051117.

Rankin, H. D. 1987. *Celts and the Classical World*. London: Croom Helm and Sydney: Areopagitica Press.

Rascovan, N. et al. 2019. Emergence and Spread of Basal Lineages of *Yersinia pestis* during the Neolithic Decline. *Cell* 176: 295–305. https://doi.org/10.1016/j.cell.2018.11.005.

Rasmussen, M. et al. 2010. Ancient human genome sequence of an extinct Palaeo- Eskimo. *Nature* Vol. 463:757–62.

Rasmussen, S. et al. 2015. Early Divergent Strains of *Yersinia pestis* in Eurasia 5,000 Years Ago. *Cell*. https://doi.org/10.1016/j.cell.2015.10.009.

Rebay-Salisbury, C. 2011. Thoughts in Circles. *Kulturkreislehre* as a Hidden Paradigm in Past and Present Archaeological Interpretations. In B. Roberts and M. Vander Linden, M., eds., *Investigating Archaeological Cultures: Material Culture, Variability and Transmission*, 41–60. Berlin: Springer.

Reher, G. S. and M. Fernández-Götz. 2015 Archaeological Narratives in Ethnicity Studies. *Archeologické rozhledy* 67: 400–16.

Reich, D. 2018. *Who We Are and How We Got Here. Ancient DNA and the New Science of the Human Past*. Oxford: Oxford University Press.

Renfrew, C. 1973. *Before Civilization. The Radiocarbon Revolution and Prehistoric Europe*. London: Jonathan Cape.

Renfrew, C. 1977. Space, Time and Polity. In J. Friedman and M. J. Rowlands, eds., *The Evolution of Social Systems*, 89–114. London: Duckworth.

Renfrew, C. 1998. From Here to Ethnicity. In J. Hall, ed., Review Feature: Ethnic Identity in Greek Antiquity. *Cambridge Archaeological Journal* 8.2: 275–7.

Renfrew, C. 2000. Commodification and Institution in Group-Oriented and Individualizing Societies. In W. G. Runciman, ed., *The Origin of Human Social Institutions*, 93–117. Oxford: Oxford University Press.

Ribeiro, A. 2019. Science, Data, and Case-Studies under the Third Science Revolution. Some Theoretical Considerations. *Current Swedish Archaeology* 27: 115–32. https://doi.org/10.37718/CSA.2019.06.

Roberts, B. and M. Vander Linden, eds. 2011. *Investigating Archaeological Cultures. Material Culture, Variability and Transmission*. Berlin: Springer.

Roberts, N. et al. 2018. Europe's Lost Forests. A Pollen-Based Synthesis for the Last 11, 000 Years. *Nature Communications* 8.716. https://doi.org/10.1038/s41598-017-18646-7.

Roberts, N. et al. 2019. Mediterranean Landscape Change during the Holocene: Synthesis, Comparison and Regional Trends in Population, Land Cover and Climate. *The Holocene* 29: 923–37. https://doi.org/10.1177/09596836 19826697.

Rowlands, M. 1980. Kinship, Alliance and Exchange in the European Bronze Age. In J. Barrett and R. Bradley, eds., *Settlement and Society in the British Later Bronze Age*, 15–55. BAR British Series 83. Oxford: Archaeopress.

Rowlands, M. and D. Fuller. 2018. Deconstructing Civilisation: A "Neolithic" Alternative. In K. Kristiansen, T. Lindkvist, and J. Myrdal, eds., *Trade and Civilisation. Economic Networks and Cultural Ties, from Prehistory to the Early Modern Era*, 172–94. Cambridge: Cambridge University Press.

Runciman, W. G., ed. 2001. *The Origin of Human Social Institutions*. Oxford: Oxford University Press.

Sahlins, M. 1968. *Tribesmen*. New Jersey: Prentice Hall.

Sahlins, M. 1972. *Stone Age Economics*. Chicago: Aldine Atherton.

Sahlins, M. 2010. The Whole is a Part: Intercultural Politics of Order and Change. In T. Otto and N. Bubandt, eds., *Experiments in Holism: Theory and Practice in Contemporary Anthropology*, 102–26. Wiley-Blackwell.

Samida, S. and M. K. H. Eggerts. 2013. *Archäologie und Naturwissenschaft? Eine Streitschrift*. Berlin: Vergangenheitsverlage.

Sánchez-Quinto, F. et al. 2019. Megalithic Tombs in Western and Northern Neolithic Europe Were Linked to a Kindred Society. *PNAS* 116.19. https://doi .org/10.1073/pnas.1818037116.

Schnapp, A. and Kristiansen, K. 1999. Discovering the Past. In G. Barker, ed., *Companion Encyclopedia of Archaeology*, 3–47. London: Routledge. https:// doi.org/10.1080/03014460.2021.1942984.

Shanks, M. and C. Tilley. 1987a. *Re-constructing Archaeology. Theory and Practice*. Cambridge: Cambridge University Press.

Shanks, M. and C. Tilley. 1987b. *Social Theory and Archaeology*. Oxford: Polity Press.

Shnirelman, V. A. 2001. *The Value of the Past: Myths, Identity and Politics in Transcaucasia*. Snri Ethnological Studies no 57. Osaka: National Museum of Ethnology.

Schroeder, H. et al. 2019. Blood Ties: Unravelling Ancestry and Kinship in a Late Neolithic Mass Grave. *PNAS* 116.22: 10705–10710. https://doi.org/10 .1073/pnas.1820210116.

Schwerin von Krosigk, H. 1982. Gustaf' Kossinna. Der Nachlass. Versuch einer Analyse. Neumunster: Wachholtz.

Service, E. R. 1962. *Primitive Social Organization. An Evolutionary Perspective*. Studies in Anthropology. New York: Random House.

Service, E. R. 1975. *Origins of the State and of Civilization. The Process of Cultural Evolution*. New York: W. W. Norton.

Shennan, S. 1978. Archaeological "Cultures": An Empirical Investigation. In I. Hodder, ed., *The Spatial Organisation of Culture*, 113–140. London: Duckworth.

Shennan, S., ed. 1989. *Archaeological Approaches to Cultural Identity*. London: Unwin Hyman.

Shennan, S. 2002. *Genes, Memes and Human History. Darwinian Archaeology and Cultural Evolution*. London: Thames & Hudson.

Shennan, S. 2018. *The First Farmers of Europe. An Evolutionary Perspective*. Cambridge: Cambridge University Press.

Shennan, S. et al. 2013. Regional Population Collapse Followed Initial Agriculture Booms in Mid-Holocene Europe. *Nature Communications* 4: 2486. https://doi.org/10.1038/ncomms3486.

Silliman, S. W. 2015. A Requiem for Hybridity? The Problem with Frankensteins, Purées, and Mules. *Journal of Social Archaeology* 15.3: 1–13.

Sinha, S. and R. Varma. 2015. Marxism and Postcolonial Theory: What is Left of the Debate? *Critical Sociology*: 1–14.

Sjögren, K.-G. et al. 2009. Megaliths and Mobility in South-Western Sweden. Investigating Relationships between a Local Society and Its Neighbours Using Strontium Isotopes. *Journal of Anthropological Archaeology* 28: 85–101.

Sjögren, K.-G. et al. 2016. Diet and Mobility in the Corded Ware of Central Europe. *PloS ONE* 11.5: e0155083. https://doi.org/10.1371/journal.pone .0155083.

Sjögren, K.-G. et al. 2021. Kinship and Social Organization in Copper Age Europe. A Cross-Disciplinary Analysis of Archaeology, DNA, Isotopes, and Anthropology from Two Bell Beaker Cemeteries. *Plos ONE*.

Smith, M., ed. 2012. *The Comparative Archaeology of Complex Societies*. Cambridge: Cambridge University Press.

Snow, C. P. 1959. *The Two Cultures and the Scientific Revolution*. Cambridge: Cambridge University Press.

Sørensen, T, F. 2017a. The Two Cultures and a World Apart: Archaeology and Science at a New Crossroads. *Norwegian Archaeological Review* 50.2. https://doi.org/10.1080/00293652.2017.1367031.

Sørensen, T. F. 2017b. Archaeological Paradigms: Pendulum or Wrecking Ball? *Norwegian Archaeological Review* 50.2 (a response to commentators). DOI: 10.1080/00293652.2017.1388274.

Sørensen, T. F. 2018. The Triviality of the New. Innovation and Impact in Archaeology and Beyond. *Current Swedish Archaeology* 26: 93–117.

Sorrano, G. et al. 2021. The Genetic and Cultural Impact of the Steppe Migration into Europe. *Annals of Human Biology* 48(3), 223–33. https://doi .org/10.1080/03014460.2021.1942984.

Sperber, L. 1999. Zu den Schwertgräbern im westlichen Kreis der Urnenfelderkultur: profane und religiöse Aspekte. In *Eliten in der Bronzezeit. Ergebnisse zweier Kolloquien in Mainz und Athen*, 605–60. Römisch-Gemanisches Zentralmuseum, Forschungsinstitut für Vor-und Frühgescichte. Bonn: Habelt.

Stig Sørensen, M. L. and C. Rebay-Salisbury. 2008. Landscapes of the Body: Burials of the Middle Bronze Age in Hungary. *European Journal of Archaeology* 11(1): 49–74. https://doi.org/10.1177/1461957108101241.

Stockhammer, P.W. 2012. Conceptualizing Cultural Hybridization in Archaeology, 43–58. In P. W. Stockhammer, ed., *Conceptualizing Cultural Hybridization: A Transdisciplinary Approach*. New York: Springer.

Stockhammer, P. W. 2022. Fostering Women and Mobile Children in Final Neolithic and Early Bronze Age Central Europe. In K. Kristiansen, G. Kroonen, and E. Willerslev, eds., *The Indo-European Puzzle Revisited*. Cambridge: Cambridge University Press.

Strien, H.-C. 2017. Group Affiliation and Mobility in the Linear Pottery Culture. In S. Scharl and B. Gehlen, eds., *Mobility in Prehistoric Sedentary Societies*, 135–44. Rahden: Verlag Marie Leidorf.

Sugita, S. 2007. Theory of Quantitative Reconstruction of Vegetation I: Pollen from Large Sites REVEALS Regional Vegetation Composition. *The Holocene* 17.2: 229–41. https://doi.org/10.1177/0959683607075837.

Sykes, N. et al. 2019. Beyond Curse or Blessing: The Opportunities and Challenges of aDNA Analysis. *World Archaeology* 51.4: 503–16. https://doi.org/10.1080/00438243.2019.1741970.

Szécsényi-Nagy, A. et al. 2014. Ancient DNA Evidence for a Homogeneous Maternal Gene Pool in Sixth Millennium Cal BC Hungary and the Central European LBK. In A. Whittle and P. Bickle, eds., *Early Farmers. The View from Archaeology and Science*. Proceedings of the British Academy 198, 71–93. Oxford: The British Academy and Oxford University Press.

Szécsényi-Nagy, A. et al. 2015. Tracing the Genetic Origin of Europe's First Farmers Reveals Insights into Their Social Organization. *Proc. R. Soc. B* 282: 20150339. http://dx.doi.org/10.1098/rspb.2015.0339

Tilley, C. 1994. *A Phenomenology of Landscape. Places, Paths and Monuments*. Oxford: Berg.

Toulmin, S. and J. Goodfield. 1965. *The Discovery of Time*. Chicago: University of Chicago Press.

Tylor, E. B. 1871. *Primitive Culture. Researches into the Development of Mythology, Philosophy, Religion, Art, and Custom*. London: Cambridge University Press.

Van Dommelen, P. 2005. Colonial Interactions and Hybrid Practices. Phoenician and Carthaginian Settlement in the Ancient Mediterranean. In G. Stein, ed., *The Archaeology of Colonial Encounters: Comparative Perspectives*, 109–41. School of American Research Advanced Seminars Series. Santa Fe, NM: School of American Research.

Van Dommelen, P. and B. Knapp, eds. 2010. *Material Connections in the Ancient Mediterranean. Mobility, Materiality and Identity*. London: Routledge.

Vandkilde, H. 1999. Social Distinction and Ethnic Reconstruction in the Earliest Danish Bronze Age. In *Eliten der Bronzezeit*, 245–76. Römisch-Germanisches Zentralmuseum Mongrafien Band 43.1. Bonn: R. Habelt.

Veeramah, K. R. 2018. The Importance of Fine-Scale Studies for Integrating Paleogenomics and Archaeology. *Current Opinion in Genetics & Development* 53: 83–9.

Veit, U. 1989. Ethnic Concepts in German Prehistory: A Case Study on the Relationship between Cultural Identity and Objectivity. In S. Shennan, ed.,

Archaeological Approaches to Cultural Identity, 35–56. London: Unwin and Hyman, Routledge.

Wahl, J. and T. D. Price. 2013. Local and Foreign Males in a Late Bronze Age Cemetery at Neckarsuhm, Southwestern Germany: Strontium Isotope Investigations. *Anthropologischer Anzeiger* 70.3: 289–307.

Wels-Weyrauch, U. 1989. Mittelbronzezeitliche Frauentrachten in Süddeutschland (Beziehungen zur Hannover Gruppierung). In *Dynamique du bronze moyen Europe occidentale*, 119–33. Paris: CTHS Edition.

Wels-Weyrauch, U. 2011. Colliers nur zur Zierde? In U. L. Dietz and A. Jockenhövel, eds., *Bronzen in Spannungsfeld zwischen praktischer Nutzung und symbolischer Bedeutung*. Praehistorische Bronzefunde Abteilung XX, 13. Band. Stuttgart: Franz Steiner Verlag.

White, H. 1987. *The Content of the Form. Narrative Discourses and Historical Representation*. Baltimore: Johns Hopkins University Press.

Wiegel, B. 1992–4. Trachtkreise im südlichen Hügelgräberbereich. Studien zur Beigabensitte der Mittelbronzezeit unter besonderer Berücksichtigung for-schungsgeschichtlicher Aspekte. Internationale Archäologie Band 5. Rahden: Verlag Marie Leidorf.

Wilkin, S. et al. 2021. Dairying Enabled Early Bronze Age Yamnanya Steppe Expansions. *Nature*: 1–5.

Witmore, T. 2014. Archaeology and the New Materialisms. *Journal of Contemporary Archaeology* 1.2: 203–46. www.pnas.org/cgi/doi/10.1073/pnas.1706416114.

Witzel, M. 2012. The Home of the Aryans. In A. Hinze and E. Tichy, eds., *Anusantatyi: Festschrift fuer Johanna Narten zum 70. Geburtstag*. Münchener Studien zur Sprachwissenschaft, Beihefte NF 19, 283–338. Dettelbach: J. H. Roell.

Žegarac, A. et al. 2021. Ancient Genomes Provide Insights into Family Structure and the Heredity of Social Status in the Early Bronze Age of Southeastern Europe. *Nature Scientific Reports* 11: 10072. https://doi.org/10.1038/s41598-021-89090-x.

Acknowledgements

This book was written to meet the theoretical and methodological challenge raised by the third science revolution and its implications for how to study and interpret European prehistory. The first part is therefore devoted to a historical and theoretical discussion of how to practice interdisciplinarity in this new age and, following from that, how to define some crucial but undertheorized categories, such as culture, ethnicity, and various forms of migration. My examples focus primarily on those periods and regions where we have seen new results from archaeogenetics and strontium and lead isotope analyses, as well as new environmental studies. It implies that the Mediterranean region is less well covered, whereas central, eastern, and northern Europe has seen many new studies of both ancient DNA and strontium and lead isotopes. So far, genetics has been faster to communicate its results to a popular audience, in books by David Reich (*Who We Are and How We Got Here*) and Johannes Krause (*Die Reise unserer Gene*). However, there is a need to integrate the new results into an archaeological frame of reference, to produce a new and theoretically informed historical narrative – one that invites further debate and also identifies areas of uncertainty where more research is needed.

However, it is also clear that I apply a specific theoretical framework that combines elements from Materialist, Marxist theory with elements from World System theory, integrated through a comparative anthropological approach toward human history, with a strong emphasis on the role of institutions in building and maintaining societies past and present. This favors a top-down approach to interpretation, which I counterbalance by employing in-depth local case studies whenever possible.

My interpretations are the outcome of more than ten years of intense collaboration with the research team at the Lundbeck Foundation Geogenetics Centre at Copenhagen University, led by Professor Eske Willerslev; the strontium researchers Karin Frei and Douglas Price with their teams; archaeologists Karl-Göran Sjögren, Sophie Bergerbrant, Serena Sabatini, and Anne Lene Melheim from the University of Gothenburg (now Oslo); archaeologist Anders Fischer; and historical linguist Guus Kroonen and his team, plus a large number of colleagues who provided not only samples but also their expertise and interpretations. From our long-lasting collaboration with the Danish National Museum, I wish to thank Poul Otto Nielsen, Lasse Sørensen, and Flemming Kaul, as well as Rune Iversen (Copenhagen University) and Niels Johansen (Aarhus University); from the Panum Institute, Niels Lynnerup and Marie-Louise

Jørkov. With all of them, I have enjoyed many inspiring workshops and meetings along the way, and I wish to thank them all, named and unnamed.

It all started back in 2010. That year we published a synthesis of three major field projects I had been involved in between 1998 and 2007 in Sicily, Hungary, and Tanum in western Sweden. I now wanted to move in new directions and had in 2009 applied for an ERC Advanced Grant, making it to the final round but not getting it. I realized the project needed something more innovative, and that had to be linked to the new breakthrough of next-generation sequencing in ancient DNA. With Per Persson and also collaborating with Anders Götherström, I had previously started an aDNA laboratory in Gothenburg (funded by the Knut and Alice Wallenberg Foundation) during the late 1990s. However, it was too early – we could not get around the problems of contamination – and we decided to close after four years of work and experimentation. Now, in 2010, the situation had radically changed, and Eske Willerslev in Copenhagen had just published the first full prehistoric genome in *Nature*. I invited Eske, who had founded the Centre for Geogenetics in Copenhagen, to join my application as partner, and we succeeded. It became the start of a fantastic and still ongoing journey.

I am deeply indebted to a large number of people with whom I have collaborated during the last ten years or more at Geogenetics. I want especially to thank Morten Allentoft, Martin Sikora, Simon Rasmussen, Peter Damgård, Fabrice Demeter, Fernando Racimo, Rasmus Nielsen, Kurt Kjær, Thomas Werge, Fulya Eylem Yediay, and Jialu Cao; on the lab side, Jesper Stenderup, and Lasse Winner; and Line Olsen for coordinating us all. Morten and Martin have been close collaborators, resulting in a series of pathbreaking papers (Allentoft et al. 2015; Allentoft et al. 2022; Rasmussen et al. 2015). Finally, I wish to thank my linguist colleagues from Copenhagen for the inspiration received on Indo-European languages, a collaboration going back several decades but renewed and intensified during the last eight to ten years, especially with Birgit Rasmussen, Thomas Olander, and Guus Kroonen. Not least has Guus been a partner in my latest project (Rise II), together with Karin Frei and Eske Willerslev, where we included the role of Indo-European languages, and this has led to many new insights (Kristiansen, Kroonen, and Willerslev 2022).

At the Department of Historical Studies in Gothenburg I wish to thank all of my colleagues – in addition to those already mentioned, Johan Ling, Christian Horn, and Bettina Schulz Paulson especially – for creating an inspiring Neolithic and Bronze Age research environment. For transforming my hand-drawn sketches into nice illustrations on short notice, I am deeply indebted to Rich Potter, who did all illustrations for this book. I also wish to stress the qualified administrative help I have always received, from Jennie Fälth especially, as well as from the leadership of first Göran Malmstedt, followed by

Helene Whittaker and now Henrik Janson. I owe a special debt to Karl-Göran Sjögren. We have collaborated more or less continuously on various projects since I became professor in 1994, where he has been an indispensable partner with expertise in several of the fields I was less familiar with, from database construction to strontium and diet studies. Here, I also need to express my gratitude for the continued and inspired collaboration I have enjoyed during the last forty years with Timothy Earle and Michael Rowlands; their vast comparative knowledge has always been a source of inspiration.

In the Element, I have freely used smaller and larger bits of text from previously published work or work in press, both by myself and from coauthored papers. For the historical background in the first section, I draw on a chapter in press titled "A History of Interdisciplinarity in Archaeology: The Three Science Revolutions, Their Implementation and Impact," to appear in the *Handbook for a History of Archaeology*, edited by Laura Coltofean-Arizancu and Margarita Díaz-Andreu. For the discussion on "The Danger of Ideological Misrepresentation" and "Toward a New Interdisciplinarity," I draw on the introductory chapter coauthored with Guus Kroonen in our forthcoming book *The Indo-European Puzzle Revisited: Integrating Archaeology, Genetics, and Linguistics*, to appear with Cambridge University Press. "The Challenge in front of Us" in the second section and "Mobility and Migration" in the third section are drawn from a chapter in press in *Homo Migrans: Modeling Mobility and Migration in Human History*, edited by Megan Daniels. Finally, in the third section, my case studies on ethnicity are drawn from a previously published paper from a volume edited by Jeremy McInerney, *A Companion to Ethnicity in the Ancient Mediterranean* (Kristiansen 2014a).

I am also indebted to colleagues who read and commented on various parts of the manuscript. They include Fernando Racimo, Steve Shennan, Mark Thomas, Guus Kroonen, Volker Heyd, Philipp Stockhammer, and Karl-Göran Sjögren.

During the last ten years, I have been fortunate to receive important research grants at the right time: first, an ERC Advanced Grant (2011–16) with the short title "The Rise" (or just Rise I); then, a major grant from the Swedish Riksbank Foundation (Rise II, Towards a New European Prehistory), running from 2017 to the end of 2022; and finally, an ERC Synergy Grant, "Corex" (from correlation to explanation, in a collaboration between UCL, Copenhagen, and Gothenburg), now running from 2021–7. I am deeply indebted to the European Research Council and the Swedish Riksbank Foundation, whose existence over the past twenty years has had a profound effect on the development of an interdisciplinary and international profile for archaeology in Europe and in Sweden. All of my projects are based on interdisciplinary collaborations between archaeology, aDNA, and strontium analyses, as well as historical linguistics and now most recently also environmental DNA. On a more practical level, I am indebted to the

Lundbeck Foundation Geogenetics Centre for sequencing hundreds or even thousands of prehistoric human samples based on grants from the Lundbeck Foundation, the Wellcome Trust, and the Novo Foundation, projects I am also taking part in that thus create new synergies between all mentioned projects. Finally, I am indebted to Copenhagen University, Faculty of Health, for granting me a five-year period as affiliated professor, and the Carlsberg foundation, for providing one of their wonderful apartments for foreign researchers during a three-year period, even if cut short by coronavirus restrictions.

Innovative research does not emerge by itself, even if resources and researchers are available. It demands a research environment that is open, free-spirited, and truly interdisciplinary. Since 2011, I have been fortunate to be a member of such a research environment created by Eske Willerslev at the Lundbeck Foundation Geogenetics Centre in Copenhagen. He is a free spirit who invites discussion, who genuinely believes in interdisciplinary collaboration, and who is constantly willing to go beyond established truths, while maintaining the highest scientific standards.

The time since 2011 has been the most exciting in my archaeological life, and the next ten years look equally promising. All of this is due not least to the inspired and generous partnership with Eske and the continued support and inspiration from Lotte, my wife, love, archaeological partner, and life companion.

Cambridge Elements ☰

The Archaeology of Europe

Manuel Fernández-Götz

University of Edinburgh

Manuel Fernández-Götz is Reader in European Archaeology and Head of the Archaeology Department at the University of Edinburgh. In 2016 he was awarded the prestigious Philip Leverhulme Prize. His main research interests are Iron Age and Roman archaeology, social identities and conflict archaeology. He has directed fieldwork projects in Spain, Germany, the United Kingdom and Croatia.

Bettina Arnold

University of Wisconsin–Milwaukee

Bettina Arnold is a Full Professor of Anthropology at the University of Wisconsin– Milwaukee and Adjunct Curator of European Archaeology at the Milwaukee Public Museum. Her research interests include the archaeology of alcohol, the archaeology of gender, mortuary archaeology, Iron Age Europe and the history of archaeology.

About the Series

Elements in the Archaeology of Europe is a collaborative publishing venture between Cambridge University Press and the European Association of Archaeologists. Composed of concise, authoritative, and peer-reviewed studies by leading scholars, each volume in this series will provide timely, accurate, and accessible information about the latest research into the archaeology of Europe from the Paleolithic era onwards, as well as on heritage preservation.

E A A | European Association *of* Archaeologists

Cambridge Elements ☰

The Archaeology of Europe

Printed in the United States
by Baker & Taylor Publisher Services